Women, Work and Development, 2

From peasant girls
to Bangkok masseuses

Pasuk Phongpaichit

International Labour Office   Geneva

ISBN 92-2-103013-X
ISSN 0253-2042

First published 1982
Fourth impression 1988

Printed in Switzerland

VAU

PREFACE

The World Employment Conference in June 1976 noted that women constitute the group at the bottom of the ladder in many developing countries, in respect of employment, poverty, education, training and status. Concerning rural women, the Conference recommended that measures be taken to relieve their work burden and drudgery by improving working and living conditions, as well as by providing more resources for investment. In order to contribute to information on work patterns and problems of rural women, part of the ILO's activities under the World Employment Programme focuses on these questions, largely through field studies by researchers in Third World countries. The aim has been gradually to develop a substantial body of knowledge and then proceed to the discussion and dissemination of research findings at seminars and workshops, followed by the planning and implementation of technical co-operation projects, in close consultation, where possible, with rural women's own organisations.

The present study is concerned with the work and lives of girls who come from rural areas to Bangkok to participate in the prostitution trade. It was carried out within the framework of an ILO World Employment Programme project on rural development and women, financed by the Federal Republic of Germany, in Asia, Africa and Latin America.

The results of in-depth interviews with 50 Bangkok masseuses are presented. The girls come from depressed rural areas; they continue to maintain strong links with their families, supplying remittances which have contributed substantially to meeting the basic needs of their families for housing, water and education, but little to productive investment in rural areas. The ability of families to send a succession of daughters to Bangkok, where they can earn as much as 25 times more than they could by labouring in a factory, has reinforced a preference for daughters.

This study concludes by explaining the place of this business in the over-all pattern of Thai economic development. As Professor Phongpaichit, the author, explains, these girls -

... were not fleeing from a family background or rural society which oppressed women in conventional ways. Rather, they were engaging in an entrepreneurial move designed to sustain the family units of a rural economy which was coming under increasing pressure. They did so, because their accustomed position in that rural society allocated them a considerable responsibility for earning income to sustain the family. The returns available in this particular business, rather than in any other business accessible to an unskilled and uneducated person, had a powerful effect on their choices. Our survey clearly showed that the girls felt they were making a perfectly rational decision within the context of their particular social and economic situation. The girls did not make the economic structure; and they could not escape from it.

This study makes a substantial contribution to the understanding of a highly publicised but under-researched dimension of women's work.

Employment and Development Department,
International Labour Office.

FOREWORD

This is a study of peasant girls who migrate into the city of Bangkok to become "masseuses". The study focuses on the causes of migration, the experience of the girls involved, and the impact on the families which they leave behind in the village. The study attempts to view this particular social group within the historical pattern of development and social change in Thailand.

The study focuses on the masseuses or "massage girls", who form one particular sector of a larger "trade". These girls work in massage parlours, of which there are at least 120 in Bangkok. Prostitution is officially illegal in Thailand, but the massage parlours offer one way in which prostitution may flourish under a thin disguise. The city also contains a large number of bars, tea houses and hotels, which also provide working space for call-girls who do not bother with the veneer of massage. Many of these bars specialise in the foreign tourist trade. The patrons of massage, however, include a large proportion of Thais.

For the girls, the massage parlour provides a society and an environment which is often safer and more comfortable than other forms of organised prostitution. The girls do not need pimps, with all the problems that they inevitably cause, and they have the usual forms of protection organised by the parlour. The girls are sometimes trained in massage, albeit in a rather rudimentary way. The practice of massage is an old Thai art, backed up by traditional medical science and believed to have considerable therapeutic value. Such traditional massage was performed "dry", but the modern massage parlour has borrowed from the Turkish bath to create a particularly lubricious version of bodily manipulation. Presumably, the pretence of offering therapeutic services was originally necessary to get round the anti-prostitution laws, but nowadays there is little attempt to disguise what the rash of recently built and often magnificently ostentatious massage parlours have to offer.

The study was conducted through interviews at massage parlours in Bangkok, and through field trips to the villages of origin of some of the girls. Fifty girls were interviewed in depth in Bangkok, and five villages were visited upcountry. These villages were situated in the North and North-east regions of the country. Within these two regions there are some villages that are well-known for sending a large number of girls to Bangkok, while in the other villages the trade may be much less, but nevertheless present. We studied villages of both types. The second section of this paper presents the material from the Bangkok survey; the third section covers the upcountry investigations; and the fourth section discusses the relationship of this migration stream to the context of Thailand's development. First, however, it is necessary to introduce the women of rural Thailand, particularly from the North and North-east regions.

TABLE OF CONTENTS

CHAPTER 1

THE VILLAGE, THE CITY AND SOCIAL CHANGE

Thailand has experienced rapid urbanisation in recent years. In fact the urban population nearly doubled between 1970 and 1980, rising from 13 per cent to 23 per cent of the total. None the less, the Thai remain an overwhelmingly rural people, and it is to the village society that one must look in order to understand the significance of urbanisation for the society as a whole as well as the socio-economic origins of female migrant streams and the basis for their adaptation to the various economic opportunities available to them in the city.

It is useful to distinguish between the social and ecological features of the Central Plain region, which constitutes the political and economic heartland of the country and the outlying North, North-east and Southern regions. The Central Plain is a relatively new and demographically fluid area. It was probably still rising out of the sea on the alluvial deposits of the Chao Phraya River when the Thai population began trickling in from southern China in significant numbers in the fourteenth century. When Thailand began, under British prodding, to emerge as a major producer and exporter of rice in the late nineteenth century, the Central Plain became an enormous and comparatively prosperous paddy field. It sucked in new population, built up a net of communications and marketing towns, benefited from intermittent addition of new irrigation schemes, and prospered. In contrast, the outlying area to the South produces tin and rubber and has a similar ethnic and economic base to that of the Malay Peninsula. The North forms part of the same hilly system as Northern Burma and Yunnan, while the North-east is an upland plain which merges into Laos and Kampuchea. Despite many differences, the outlying areas are alike in being poorer than the Central Plain and in having local cultures and social systems which have been less disrupted in recent centuries by prosperity, mobility and urbanisation.

The anthropological literature on Thai social structure, family, marriage and the position of women is confused and full of controversy. Perhaps because earlier studies focused on the fluid society of the Central Plain, and because Thai practices did not fit into the rigid hierarchical and predominantly patrilineal models

observed in tribal and peasant societies elsewhere in Asia and
Africa, Thai society came to be described as "loosely structured".[1]
Recent investigations carried out in villages of the North and
North-east, however, have shown that while there might be no strong
lineage-based groups there are, nevertheless, powerful social
structures organised around affinal relations, and these groupings
can only be understood through the role of women.[2]   The family,
as well as larger groupings of families within the village, are
structured around the female members.   Within each family unit,
authority rests with the senior male.   This authority does not
pass from father to son, but is transmitted through the female line.
At marriage a man leaves his own natal family and, through contribution of his own labour to the bride's family and payment of at least
a token brideprice, joins the ritual, economic and social group of
his wife and her sisters.   At the death of the senior male, the
family property is shared equally between sons and daughters, but
the family home is customarily allotted to the youngest daughter
who is expected to look after the parents in old age.   The attach-
ment of women to their family group gave them and their children
some insurance against the loss of husbands and other male members,
whether by disease, death in military service, abandonment, or some
other misfortune - and such loss is apparently not uncommon.
Family groupings based on matrilateral ties sometimes operate
systems of labour sharing, and are bound together by shared ritual
practices.   Women also play a large role in ritual and many of the
most authoritative and powerful spirits are female.[3]

Of special importance to understanding modern patterns of
migration of rural women from these areas in the North and North-
east is the economic responsibility imposed on them by their
traditional social role.   Both women and men are expected to
contribute to the household's productive activities, but it is the
women who are expected to manage the finances of the family.   A
dividing line exists between "women's work" and "men's work" but it
is flexible.   A woman, for instance, would not normally handle the
plough, but in cases where the family has no men around to carry out
the ploughing then the women will do it.   The distinct femininity
of village women is recognised and greatly valued, but in practice
is expressed in terms of protecting themselves from the sun when
working in the field rather than excluding women from such work
responsibilities.

Thai women as a whole have a remarkably high rate of participation in the labour force. According to the 1970 census and the
1978 labour force survey, the number of women in employment was
about 70 per cent of the number of men, or about two-thirds of all
adult women. Both surveys, however, were conducted during the
agricultural off-season, hence excluding casual or underemployed
workers from the category of the employed. If we add the enormous
number described as "waiting for the agricultural season" to the
category of employed, the ratio of women to men in employment would
be between 83 and 87 per cent. Only 16 to 17 per cent of women
over 11 years (excluding students) describe themselves as house-
workers. In the rural sector, women participate equally with men
in the primary sector and outnumber men by almost two to one in
trade. In urban Thailand, women are again prominent in trade,
professional jobs, and services and to some extent also in industry.
Administrative jobs, particularly those in government, are dominated
by men, but it is far from uncommon to find a family where the
husband is a government officer and the wife runs a shop or business.

The relationship between man and woman in the court and aristocracy was always very different compared to that in the village.
Thai monarchs absorbed elements of Brahminical culture to provide
the kind of backing for a divinely-ordained kingship which was
conspicuously lacking in Buddhism.[4] Brahminical ideas also supplied
ideological support for male supremacy on a wider scale. As in many
aristocratic cultures, the women of the court were expected to func-
tion as decorative status symbols rather than productive workers,
while the women of lower rank were often prey to some form of droit-
de-seigneur.[5] The result was a culture of male dominance in which
polygamy and concubinage played a significant role.

The commercialisation of rice trade in the late nineteenth
century and expansion of the export economy were accompanied by a
large-scale influx of immigrant trading communities. The values
and practices regarding sexual roles and marriage systems of these
communities were very different from those of traditional rural Thai
society, and their spread brought the practice of polygamy and
concubinage closer to the ordinary people. Women were expected to
play a submissive and non-productive role, male ancestors were
worshipped, the importance of bearing sons was stressed, and elaborate
marriage ceremonies and the payment of dowry were introduced.[6]
Prostitution was also introduced on a large scale for the first time,

in part due to the predominance of young males within the long-distance migration streams. The Sampeng area behind the port in Bangkok soon became both the city's immigrant ghetto and its red-light district. Polygamy and the collection of concubines became part of the status symbolism of being wealthy. In this period the Thai nobility also became more expansive and more public about the multiplication of consorts, elaborating a complex system of graded wives and concubines.[7] The values and practices of the rich and powerful provided a model for aspirant members of the new urban populations as the towns and cities began to grow in the early twentieth century.

The growth of urban Thailand thus saw two important developments in sexual politics. First, prostitution significantly expanded. Second, the right of the rich and powerful to take many consorts acquired a kind of public legitimacy.

In the era of high colonialism from the late nineteenth century to the 1930s, Thailand was not brought under formal foreign rule but was none the less subjected to many of the stresses and strains of colonial societies. The commercial economy grew under European prodding, and the Government was haltingly "modernised" under foreign tutelage. When the depression of the 1930s sent a tremor through the whole colonial system, Thailand experienced a political revolution which brought new social groups into the political forefront. The groups, which came to prominence in the 1930s and dominated politics until the 1950s, were bureaucrats and military officers. As revolutions go, however, it was slow and incomplete and the doyens of this new ruling group aspired to many of the same marks of status that had characterised the old order. The late 1950s and 1960s saw the other major product of post-colonial society, the commercial class, brought forward to share prominence with the bureaucrats and military leaders.[8] Although an act was passed banning prostitution and countless campaigns were waged to check the import of "Western permissiveness" there seemed to be little relationship between the "private" life of the new elite and their public aspirations.

The association of power and profit with the amassing of wives and consorts remains a model to which many aspire. Indeed, for many successful business families, expansion depends almost wholly on the supply of trustworthy managerial personnel (and that means sons). The big business families of Bangkok are famous for their average number of wives, and a successful entrepreneur-patriarch can usually hope to count his grandchildren in a three-digit number.

In the post-revolution years, another form of sexual exploita-
tion came into prominence, namely the institution of the beauty
contest.   Girls from the North were especially successful, earning
the region and even particular villages a special kind of distinction.   These aesthetic battles received prominent coverage in the
press and became showcases where prominent political figures could
select their consorts.

The presence of foreign military personnel in Asia during a
succession of wars in recent decades, and with a paypacket so
enormously fatter than the average local income, helped to spread
prostitution.[9]   In the late 1960s it was estimated that these short-
term visitors spent about 400 million baht annually,[10] an amount
roughly equivalent to the aggregate (average) income of a quarter of
a million Thai people.   With the end of these wars, the service
industries did not decline as might have been expected, however, but
rather expanded, based not only on local demand but also the growth
of tourism.   The number of tourists visiting Thailand rose from
212,000 in 1964 to 630,000 in 1970, 1,107,000 in 1975 and 1,370,000
in 1978.[11]   The sex ratio of the tourist population was conspicuously
regular at 2:1 in favour of men.   The major attractions of a trip to
Thailand were hardly obscured by those responsible for the marketing.[12]

By 1973, tourism was already providing 11 per cent of Thailand's
foreign exchange earnings.   In the late 1970s it was vying with
sugar for second place (behind rice).[13]   Embarrassment over the
country's growing reputation led to action against some agencies
running the most flagrant operations, and in early 1980 the head of
the Thai tourist authority asked the tour agencies to moderate their
emphasis on the erotic attractions of Thailand and to play up the
temples and the natural beauty of the country instead.[14]   But as
long as tourism contributes so importantly to an embattled balance
of payments position, it seems unlikely that such pleas will be
followed by more effective action.

Estimates of the proportion of young women involved in Bangkok's
night life can be, as we shall see below, quite astounding.   This
aspect of the city's life is no longer contained within an enclave,
rather it is a prominent feature of the culture of the entire city.
The business is so pervasive that it cannot help but affect the
general atmosphere and social life of the city.[15]

The evolution of the sexual service industry in Thailand must thus be seen as the result of a number of historical, economic and social factors coming together in a particular configuration. On the one hand, there is the rural society of the outlying areas which emphasises the social and economic role of women, and this combines with the pressures of poverty and seemingly unlimited earning opportunities for women through urban migration. On the other hand, there is the adaptation and historical elaboration of the marital norms and privileges of the elite. This created a culture of polygamy and concubinage which apparently legitimates the commoditisation of women. The influx of foreign military personnel associated with successive wars in the Asia arena helped to create the infrastructure for widespread prostitution, but the marketing of erotic tourism began to build upon that foundation even before this clientele began to fade away. The sexual service industry in Bangkok is thus firmly entrenched and, as we shall investigate further in the latter sections of this monograph, appears to form part of the socio-economic logic of contemporary Thailand.

CHAPTER 2

DOWNTOWN BANGKOK

At the end of the Second World War, Bangkok was still more of
an old-fashioned "port-of-trade" than a modern metropolis. The
population of around 700,000 was clustered closely around the old
"royal city" and the adjacent old commercial area of Sampeng and
Yaowarat, and a close mesh of canals provided the main means of
communication with the immediately surrounding region. Since the
1950s, the population has been growing at around 5 per cent a year,
and has sprawled way beyond the old city in a straggle of shop-
houses, factories, hotels, office blocks and garden suburbs. The
canals have mostly disappeared under tarmac, and the city has an
unmistakable, pervasive, insistent atmosphere of commerce. The
population is now over 8 million. According to one government
survey, this figure includes about 18,000 girls who work as
prostitutes or massage girls, but the authors of the survey admit
that this was only a rough count in those establishments where
they could get access.[16] Conventional estimates of the number of
masseuses and prostitutes in Bangkok start at around 100,000.
Most estimates cluster around 200,000. The total number of
masseuses, prostitutes and girls in "special services" in the whole
country is not known. But it is probably around 500,000 at
present, or about 10 per cent of the girls in the age group 14-24.
The Police Department gave a total figure of just over 400,000 in
1964.[17]

Upcountry people coming into the city inevitably finish up in
the least attractive and least remunerative occupations. Upcountry
women are even worse off than men; and uneducated or poorly
educated upcountry women have a limited and generally depressing
range of job opportunities. A recent study estimated the income
ranges of the jobs open to women in the city:

Occupation	Baht per month
Housemaid	150- 450
Waitress	200- 500
Construction labouring	200- 500
Factory employee	200- 500
Beauty salon	400- 600
Clerical work	600-1 000
Services	800-1 500

The same survey estimated the usual income of a prostitute or masseuse was around 10,000, with possibilities of substantial bonuses on top of that.[18]   In other words, the income from this line of business was about 25 times as large as the median level to be expected in other occupations.   Many girls who have a mainstream job will also peddle their bodies to earn a supplement which will bring earnings up to a more comfortable level.   A recent survey of 1,000 massage girls caused a little stir in the corridors of power when it announced that 1 per cent of the sample were moonlighting from government jobs.[19]

It might be thought that mainstream jobs would promise a longer and more secure working life, but this would probably be misleading.   Most of the available jobs entail hard labour in dreadful conditions, and ill-health or debility will cut short the working career at an unusually young age.   Until recently, some of the textile factories, for instance, which were among the biggest employers of female labour in the organised sector, had a policy to sack their women around the age of 30 because they knew that the women's absenteeism and inefficiency would soon increase dramatically as a result of lung disease and other products of the bad working conditions.[20]   Construction workers suffer in a similar way, while the demand for such workers as waitresses and beauticians drops off severely with advancing age.

The parlours

In Bangkok alone, according to a study by Dr. Thepanom of Mahidol University, there are 119 massage parlours, 119 barber-shop-cum-massage and tea-houses, 97 night-clubs, 248 disguised whore-houses and 394 discos-cum-restaurants - all of which provide similar services for male customers.[21]   In this study we looked specifically at girls from the massage parlours, although there is really no strict dividing line between the different types and different locations of work within the general business of prosti-tution.   Fifty girls were interviewed, and they were distributed over nine different massage parlours which covered all grades from the decidedly ritzy to the definitely sleazy.[22]   At the bottom of the market there are establishments which have about 30 girls and which are little different (except in name) from a regular whore-house.   At the top of the market there are establishments which have 400 regular girls, which do offer massage, and which offer a whole catalogue of other services besides.

An example of the lowest grade of parlour was sited in a three-storied shophouse down a gloomy and miry alley off one of the busy roads of Bangkok's modern business district.   The entrance leads into a bar and coffee-shop with all the usual soft lights and night-club decor.   There are several cubicles with tables and comfortable armchairs for the customers to sit and drink. Next door is a room with a glass cage and no source of natural light.   The girls sit in the cage lit by dim artificial lights. Opposite, and outside the cage, is a row of benches where the men may sit and contemplate their choice.   In some places there is a one-way mirror to ensure that the girls cannot see the clients, but in the cheaper establishments the shadows have to be enough.   The client picks out his girl by the number pinned on her blouse, and pays the appropriate rate at a desk to one side of the cage.   The clients can take the girl to drink in the coffee-shop next door, but usually they move directly upstairs. Here the pretence of the establishment's title quickly disappears.   There are no facilities for massage at all.   Most of the customers are wage labourers, drivers and other low-income young males.

The girls in such establishments are divided into two groups - the pretty and the plain - which command different rates of pay. The pretty ones cost the customer 60 baht per hour, while the not-so-pretty cost only 40. These rates vary from time to time according to the state of the economy, and during the recent drought in the countryside and credit squeeze in the urban sector, the level dropped to 50 and 30 respectively. The girls received between a quarter and a half of this fee, depending on their status in the establishment. The lower rate is applicable to the "bonded" girl, that is those who are brought to the place by a recruiting agent. An example is a girl said to be 18 years old, brought to Bangkok by an agent who "loaned" her parents ฿1,500 on the condition that their daughter would work at the parlour until the debt was cleared. Such girls live in the upstairs section of the parlour, and are heavily guarded to make sure that they do not run away before the indenture has been cleared. The parents of this particular girl came to visit her soon after she came to Bangkok in order to make sure she was in a good place. They were happy to find that their daughter was living in a concrete building with air-conditioning in the middle of town. Although the building is tucked away down a rather grotty lane, it seemed quite posh enough to the visitors from the rural North. The rest of the girls are "freelance", and they get the higher percentage (a half) of the client's fee. These are girls who have joined the parlour of their own (relatively) free will. They generally live off the premises and have to pay for their own accommodation and medical fees.

In the upmarket establishments, the presentation is very different, though of course the end product is much the same. An example is a large parlour situated in a modern district of hotels and office blocks. It is a large four-storeyed building, which announces its presence ostentatiously with gushing fountains and tall neon lights. Inside there are 400 rooms, each with a different design and decor. You can choose perhaps a room surrounded with floor-to-ceiling mirrors, or perhaps a room entirely made of imported marble, right down to the twin baths. One characteristic is, however, shared by all of the rooms. There are no windows and no source of natural light, just dim artificial illumination in all the rooms. The labour force includes 400 girls. In all of the good-grade parlours visited during the interviews, the girls were recruited at the establishment itself. A sign was hung outside to advertise vacancies. This did not mean that some of the girls working there had not originally been recruited and brought to the parlour by agents. New girls were

trained in the particular style of massage offered in these places
by a resident instructor.   The training session lasts two to three
days and costs the girl a fee of 100 baht.   Three hundred of the
girls offered the regular massage at the rate of 80 baht per hour.
The remaining hundred girls offered a special service provided in
pairs and retailed at 350 per half hour.   In both cases the girls
received 38 per cent of the customer fee.   If, following the
regular massage, the customer asked for more, then the fee would
have to be bargained out between the customer and the girl.   The
price which the girl could command for sexual intercourse would
depend entirely on her bargaining position, and the parlour-owner
would demand no cut.   Thus, in this type of parlour, the girls
would have two sources of income - the percentage of the hourly
rates for massage and the negotiable payment for any additional
services.

Some of the upmarket parlours provide the girls with accommodation and regular medical checks.   In such circumstances, the
percentage of the massage fee received by the girls would fall to
somewhere in the range of 25 to 35 per cent.   The fees payable by
the customers in different parlours ranged from 60 to 140 baht per
hour for the regular service, and from 220 to 350 per half hour
for the "sandwich course" (the local term, spoken in English, for
the tandem version).   About half of the clients in the upmarket
establishments were estimated to be foreigners, with roughly
another 30 per cent contributed by local businessmen.[23]

According to the 1960 Prostitution Act, prostitution is
illegal.   Anyone found to be engaging in the trade, including
owners of establishments, is liable to imprisonment from three
months to one year, or a fine varying from 1,000 to 2,000 baht.
If this law were strictly enforced, the masseuses, owners of
massage parlours and others involved would be fined every day, for
it can easily be proved that all these places are in fact disguised
whore-houses.   However, all the massage parlours are registered as
bars and eating places and they are well protected by local police,
who receive sufficient rewards from the owners.   The police rarely
raid a massage parlour.   If it ever happens, it is usually because
there are disputes over the protection fees.   This is widely
acknowledged, even by the police themselves.   (The author was
offered to be taken around some of these massage places with a
policeman.   Similarly, Dr. Thepanom, who made a study of the health

conditions of massage girls for UNFPA, was assisted in his interviews by high-ranking police and army officers who wrote letters asking the owners of establishments to collaborate with the study.)

There is one massage parlour in Bangkok which is especially famous. It offers only massage.

* * * *

We interviewed 50 masseuses from 9 establishments in Bangkok. Both male and female interviewers were used. It was thought that male interviewers might not get accurate answers because the girls would distort their replies to get the interviewers' sympathy, while female interviewers might get biased answers because the girls were conscious of the differences in their social status. We tried to choose interviewers who had previously visited massage parlours. This was possible among male interviewers, but not in the case of female. The author also participated in the inter- viewing. A standard rate was paid to the interviewees for their time. We did not make use of letters of introduction, in order to avoid false answers or prepared answers arranged by the owners who wanted to present a certain image of their establishments. We tried to control the sample to include only migrant girls, but this was not completely successful. It was difficult to judge the regional origin of a girl when picking her out of the glass cage. The interviewees thus include two girls who originate from Bangkok itself. The remainder were all upcountry migrants.

The masseuses

The largest proportion of the sample girls came from the North of Thailand (48 per cent), followed by the North-east (26 per cent), and the Central Plain (20 per cent), with just 2 per cent from the South. Dr. Thepanom's study of 1,000 girls found an even higher proportion from the North, that is 75 per cent. Seventy per cent of them came from farming families, while 16 per cent came from families with small trading businesses and the remainder from families of wage labourers, domestic workers, car repairers, hair- dressers and radio repairers. Among those coming from the North, all but three came from agricultural backgrounds.

As might be expected among girls from such backgrounds, they had all been introduced to work at an early age and had some experience of work before coming to Bangkok. The village occupations of the 48 migrants who had worked before moving were distributed as follows:

Occupations before leaving home of 48 migrants	Percentage
Help in the family farm	37.5
Housewives	16.7
Small trading	14.6
Students	10.4
Labourers, factory workers	6.2
Waitresses	6.2
Salesgirls	4.2
Collecting forest products	2.1

In such circumstances, few of them had managed to garner much education. Forty per cent of them had no education at all, and another 52 per cent had less than 4 years of elementary schooling; 4 per cent had 4-6 years, while only the remaining 4 per cent had made it into the secondary school.

At the same time, most of them came from large families. The number of children in the families from which the girls came was distributed as follows:

Number of children	Percentage of girls
0- 4	14
5- 7	56
8-10	26
Over 11	4

Most of the families fell in the range of 5 to 7 children, with a mean of 6.38. The families of origin thus tended to be larger than the average; the mean size of a household, including parents and possibly grandparents and other dependants, in rural Thailand is around 5.5 members.

The reason which the overwhelming majority of girls gave as the cause of migration was the desire to find work to alleviate pressing problems of poverty in the family. The answers were distributed as follows:

Reasons for migrating	Number	Percentage
Reasons connected with wanting to work and to increase family income	41	85
Studying	2	4
Following relatives	2	4
Wanting to see Bangkok	1	2
Being lured by husband	1	2
Running away because of rape	1	2
Total	48	100
Among those who moved for reasons connected with work, actual reasons cited were:		
Poverty, the family's inability to find enough food	35	85
Need of income after husband's desertion	2	5
No work at home, bad rice harvest	2	5
Want to leave husband and need income	2	5
Total	41	100

The economic incentive is patently clear. Most of the girls came from the two poorest regions of the country (the North and the North-east), and chiefly from farming families with large numbers of dependants. Most of them had left because of the pressure of poverty.

The most popular ages for leaving home were between 18 and 23, although one girl left at 12 and two more at 13 (one of whom went directly to work in a massage parlour). The distribution of ages at times of migration was as follows:

Age at migration	Number of girls
12-13	4
14-15	5
16-17	5
18-19	10
20-21	9
22-23	10
24 and over	5

Sixty-four per cent of them came directly from the village to work as masseuses.   Of these direct recruits, 46 per cent came from the North, 32 per cent from the Central Plain and 22 per cent from the North-east.   All except six got the jobs through friends and relatives who were already in the trade.   Of the remaining six, three entered the business of their own volition, while the other three were pressured by a husband, an agent and a boyfriend, respectively.

The remainder went first to other jobs in the city.   House-maid was the most common job, followed by waitressing, factory work, seamstress and salesgirl, in that order.   The wages they earned in these prior occupations were in the range of ฿300-400 a month for housemaids, ฿400-600 for waitresses, seamstresses and factory work, and ฿700-800 for salesgirls.   Twelve of them had acquired some skill as dressmakers, and another seven had skills as hair-dressers or beauticians.   But the vast majority had acquired no saleable skill or training.   Most of them drifted from these occu-pations into massage because the other occupations could not deliver an income which would allow them to live reasonably or remit money to their families.

On their route from the village to the city and into the massage parlour, many of them had abandoned a husband or lover along the way.   Sixty-six per cent had already been married, another 28 per cent were not married but had already lost their virginity before being recruited to the parlour, while 6 per cent were still virgins when they entered the trade.   The husbands included six farmers, four policemen, four traders, three drivers, two labourers, two teachers, a civil servant and a fisherman.   Of the 33 who had been married, 27 had since been divorced.   Ten of these (including

three of the four who had married policemen) cited the husband's
desertion as the reason for divorce, six mentioned incompatibility
or problems with the husband's family, while one blamed it on money
problems and another on the husband's insobriety.   Among those who
were still married, two had run away from their husbands, one was
being forced into the massage business by her husband, another had
her husband's consent, and the remaining two said that their
husbands did not know about their trade.

All of the girls were very recent migrants.   All except one
had come to Bangkok within the last five years.   The length of
time they had been working as masseuses was also in general very
short:

Length of time	Percentage
Less than 1 year	12.5
1-2 years	49.0
2-4 years	31.2
4-5 years	6.3

Forty-six per cent of the girls were now in the age range 21-25,
while 34 per cent were younger than that, 14 per cent were 26-30
and 6 per cent were over 31.   Only three of them expressed any
enthusiasm for remaining in the trade for any longer than was
necessary.   In answer to the question how long this would be, the
replies were distributed as follows:

How much longer?	Percentage
A few months	10
One year	12
2-3 years	18
4-5 years	4
5-6 years	4
Until I have earned enough	32
Don't know or other	20

Among those who asserted that they would go on until they had earned enough, two specifically mentioned debts that had to be paid off, and two mentioned the duration of a sister's education. Others had the target of building houses in the village, and having enough capital to set up a shop or other small business that would enable them to sustain their economic independence. Among the "other" reasons, two were hoping to find a husband who would relieve them of duty, while one girl said she would continue until the clients no longer wanted her.

Many of them had clear ambitions of what they wanted to do after quitting the trade, and their target of earnings was geared to this goal. The girls described the occupations they wanted to follow after quitting the parlours as follows:

Occupations	Percentage
A hairdressing shop	18
A trading shop	18
Farming	8
Be a minor wife	9
Have a dressmaking shop	4
Become a seamstress	2
Work in factory	2
Study hairdressing more	2
Don't want to quit	6
Go home/be a housewife	6
Don't know	28

Of the 17 who offered replies to this particular question, 5 thought that their history in the massage trade would impede their marriage prospects, but 11 denied it and 2 were not sure. Ten wanted to marry men from their native region, but five others were not bothered about the place of origin and five more insisted only that the husband be rich. Four had no intention of getting married at all.

The picture thus emerges of young girls from marginal rural families with large numbers of dependants. A good number also had a sad history of personal and marital relations behind them. They

came direct into the massage business, or drifted in after migrating
to other occupations, because of the considerable financial incentives that it offered.   Few like the trade, and most expect to work
for no more than a few years.   But they are either pressed by
financial imperatives, or have developed ambitions to raise enough
capital to ensure a longer-term economic survival, and this target,
rather than any time limit, circumscribes their view of the future.
The commonest ambition is to open a small business such as hair-
dressing, dressmaking or retail, and perhaps also to get married.

How long this will take, or whether the target will ever be
reached, depends upon the girl's level of income and that, as we
have already seen, differs enormously according to the girl's
talents and the grade of her establishment.   Some idea can be got,
however, from circumstantial data.   Thirty-six of the girls
talked about friends who had once been in the business and had now
quit.   Their post-parlour life had turned out as follows:

Girls who have left	Number
Married and gone to countryside	16
Married and in Bangkok	1
Married and gone abroad	2
Minor wife	2
Started hairdressing shop	2
Started other shop	5
Went home to farm	1
Coming and going*	7

(* That is, still drifting in and out of the
massage trade.)

Among girls who had left the trade and who were met later in the
village, one had managed to build a house back home within a year,
while another had stuck it out for ten years and had built two
houses and set up a business.

It is difficult to estimate the massage girls' incomes, and
pretty meaningless to compute an average.   The estimation is
difficult because of the natural tendency to conceal or distort
the actual level.   Averaging would be inappropriate because of

the wide disparity between girls working at different levels.   A
good-looking girl in a posh establishment is conventionally
reckoned to earn 25,000 a month.   A "bonded" girl in a grotty
place with a drunken and dishonest owner would be lucky to get 500.

Dr. Thepanom's study estimated an average income of 8,500 baht
a month.   The sample studied here returned incomes in the following ranges:

Masseuses' monthly income (baht)	Number	Percentage
1 000- 2 000	2	4
2 000- 3 000	6	12
3 000- 4 000	10	20
4 000- 5 000	3	6
5 000- 6 000	15	30
6 000- 7 000	4	8
7 000- 10 000	8	16
10 000- 15 000	2	4
	50	100

Over half of the girls fell into the range of B3,000-6,000 a month
with another 28 per cent earning rather more than that.   Those who
fell below B3,000 were mainly the staff of the low-grade houses, and
the "bonded" girls.

Most of the girls found Bangkok expensive, but clearly also
enjoyed the prospect of living well.   Housing they found especially
expensive.   Usually they shared a flat with other girls, which kept
the rent down to B600-1,000 a month, but one of the girls who was
particularly successful (earning B10,000-15,000) was paying B3,000
for her own flat.   More than half of the girls said they spent a
lot on cosmetics, clothing and eating out in the evening.   The
leisure activities which they volunteered range widely from tennis
(a very fashionable sport in Bangkok) and English lessons offered by
one of the more obviously successful and ambitious girls, to making
paper bags for sale.   The vast majority, however, found little or
no time for recreation.

Hobby or leisure activity	Number
Movies, "just going out"	6
Reading (usually cartoons)	5
Sport*	3
Sleeping	3
Dressmaking	2
Visiting relatives	1
Knitting	1
Going on picnics	1
Tending plants	1
Shopping	1
Housework	1
Making paper bags for sale	1
No leisure time	1
Studying to be a beautician	1
None	22

* One linked sport with studying English.

Few of the girls had any good things to say about their clients, but most of the answers betrayed resignation rather than anger.

Opinions about their clients	Number
Cannot be trusted/deceitful	10
Selfish	5
Some good, some bad	4
Nothing special/like all men	3
Boring	2
Irresponsible	1
Arrogant	1
Running away from their wives	1
Just want to go to bed	1
Come to solve their problems	1
Some of them are better than my husband	1

When asked about Thai society, the girls rendered answers which show their surprise at the blatant commercialism of Bangkok. They found the society expensive, competitive, selfish, unsafe, superficial, and hard on them in particular. One or two made an explicit comparison with the more comfortable environment of the village.

A picture emerges of a group of rather disorientated young girls, but it would be wrong to give too gloomy an impression. Some of the girls revealed to the interviewers (only to the female interviewers) that they were quite enjoying themselves. These were mainly the more beautiful and successful ones, but also those who had an unlucky marriage and were escaping from a cruel or boring husband. They had money in their pocket, they had some occasional pleasure from the work, and they had the chance to make their way in society. There were glamorous stories about the most successful massage girls, and such stories gave hope and even a kind of vicarious pride. One such story concerned a girl of such beauty that the clients had to book up weeks in advance, and queue even to get a glimpse of her. Such stories linked up with the knowledge that Thailand had a great tradition of socially mobile concubines and courtesans. There was always the chance of being swept away by some rich businessman or foreigner (there are stories of girls who were married to rich foreigners) and moved into an entirely different world.

But the hazards of the business were also clear. While some of the luckier girls were looked after medically by the better organised parlours, many of them had to pay for their own VD checks and doctors' bills. In Dr. Thepanom's sample of 1,000 girls, 41 per cent had VD. Thepanom also collected the figures of people visiting the Government's VD clinics in 1979 in 66 jangwats (districts = most of the country). In the total of 700,216 visitors, 102,440 were girls who offered "special services" (a direct translation of the Thai). Forty-nine per cent of all the tests proved positive, and 71 per cent of the men found to be suffering from VD said that they had contracted it from "special services" girls. These statistics provide a useful impression, but should not be considered exhaustive. The government hospitals would see only a small proportion of VD cases, since Bangkok and other large towns have a considerable number of private VD clinics. Thepanom's sample of 1,000 had also borne a total of 752 children. Many of the girls in our sample also had children, who were usually now under the care of a parent or other relative. Several had

also had abortions (19 per cent in Thepanom's sample), and since
abortion is still illegal in Thailand, most of these were the
back-street sort with all the dangers and subsidiary complications
that such operations always entail.   Thepanom's study also found
that a quarter of the girls were regular users of drugs, particularly barbiturates (secanol), amphetamines, and heroin.   We did
not pursue this matter in our study, but two girls mentioned that
they drank a lot, and one confessed that she was a drug addict and
had attempted suicide three times.

The home link

No more than about a quarter of the sample claimed that they
were honest with their family in telling them exactly what they
were doing in Bangkok.   Others generally told their families that
they were working in service occupations.   Noticeably, only one
had definitely severed relations with her family.   These were
definitely not runaways.   Indeed, all were sending money to them.
The dependants listed by the 46 girls nearly always included their
parents, and in 18 cases also included their own children.

Aggregate of dependants listed by 46 girls	
Grandparents	2
Parents	83
Siblings	88
Children	27
Total	200

Most of the girls still visited their home villages quite often.
The usual pattern was to visit twice a year at the major festivals,
but others went far more frequently.   Only four said that they
emphatically never went home.

Frequency of visits home	Number
Never	4
Very rarely*	4
Once a year	9
2-3 times a year	13
4-7 times a year	6
Every month	2
Several times a month	3
Often	2
When parents are sick	1
Live in Bangkok	2
Just arrived so no time yet	3
No answer	1

* One explained that she visited home rarely
because her parents were boring and her
brother invariably drunk.

All but these four girls sent money back to their homes.
Two said that the sums were irregular and according to need, but
others said that they made a fairly regular remittance.

Monthly remittances to family (in baht)	Number
None	4
- 500	6
- 1 000	17
- 1 500	3
- 2 000	10
- 2 500	2
- 3 000	4
- 6 000	1
- 10 000	1
When needed	2

The table shows maximum amounts mentioned ("- 2,000" reflects
an answer like "one to two thousand") and obviously the sums would
fluctuate according to the vagaries of supply.   Most girls claimed
to send around one-third to one-half of their earnings, and the
median amount was in the range of 1,000-2,000 baht.   Many said
they would send additional lump sums on request to cover special
outlays like medical fees, school expenses for siblings or children
and payment for hired labour during the harvest season.   Commonly
the money was used simply to supplement the inadequate amounts
available to the family for living expenses, while siblings' school
expenses also figured prominently in the answers.

Eight of the girls said they had already built a house for
their parents in the home village, while most of the girls aimed
to do so before they quit.   One girl had built two houses - one
for herself and one for her parents - and was still saving to
build a dressmakers' shop, to which she thought she would be able
to retire in two years' time.   This effort of accumulation had
taken ten years.   The other seven who had already managed to build
houses had been working for two to four years.   Houses built in
the villages cost in the range of ฿30,000-80,000.   Such a sum is
very low by the standards of Bangkok costs, because labour is cheap
and wood freely available in the village.   But it is a large sum
in terms of agricultural incomes.

In sum, the Bangkok survey found mostly girls who came from
the poor regions of the country (particularly the North), and
from hard-pressed agricultural families.   Several already had a
past of unhappy marriages and personal relations.   They usually
came to Bangkok in their teens, and were planning to work long
enough to earn a target sum.   Their incomes, opportunities and
outlooks varied very widely.   At one end of the scale were girls
who were earning very well, having a reasonable amount of glamorous
fun, cherishing the possibility of marrying well, and saving
steadily for a secure future in a small business.   At the other
end were girls who were more obviously repressed in every way.
Their incomes were low, their outlook rather bewildered, and their
health in obvious danger.   But perhaps the most remarkable thing
about the sample girls was their conception of themselves as
family breadwinners.   They were not, like so many young people
making for the bright lights of the city, extracting themselves

from their family background.   All but four retained good links
with their families and remitted money into the family exchequer.
It is now time to follow the path of the postal orders, out from
Bangkok into the villages of the Thai countryside.

CHAPTER 3

UPCOUNTRY

The North and the North-east

The North and the North-east are the two poorest regions of
the country. Geographically and culturally, each is very distinc-
tive, and the origins of their poverty are also diverse. The
North-east is a flattish upland plain, stranded in the blisteringly
dry area between the alluvial deltas of the Chao Phraya and Mekhong
rivers. Towards the east of the region, the population includes
a large number of Lao and Khmer peoples. There is little economic
activity outside agriculture. The North, by contrast, is a hilly
region with the main centres of population strung out along narrow
river valleys and elevated plateaux. There is a considerable
business of forestry as well as agriculture. The more remote
parts are still sparsely populated by hill tribes such as the
Kachin, Karen and Meo, while the bulk of the population describe
themselves as "Khon Myang" (Khon people) in rigid distinction to
the "Khon Thai" of the Central Plain, and still share much in
common with the people of Burma and Yunnan on the other slopes of
the hill ranges.

The North is marginally better off than the North-east, but
both trail behind the alluvial rice-growing tract of the Central
Plain, and well behind the metropolis of Bangkok. Estimates from
1976-78 (table 2) show that per capita GDP in the North was about
half that in the Central Plain, and a quarter that in Bangkok,
while the level in the North-east was only about three-fifths of
that in the North. Moreover the trend in these years was for the
North and North-east to be losing ground against the Central Plain
and the capital. This trend may extend back to 1962-63, according
to information from the household expenditure surveys presented
in table 3. Here the data show that the North and North-east
were marginally falling behind the city between 1962-63 and 1968-69.
The figures for 1975-76 are not at all comparable, because the
definition of Bangkok was expanded to include areas with a large
agricultural population which certainly depress the average figure.
There is also a significant gap between the ratio of North :
Bangkok and North-east : Bangkok between the 1962-63 and 1968-69
figures shown in table 3 on the one hand, and the 1976-78 figures

Table 2: GDP per capita in different regions, expressed as a
          percentage of GDP per capita in Bangkok, 1976-78

Region	1976	1977	1978
North-east	16.2	15.3	14.8
North	25.9	24.3	24.1
South	36.3	38.1	38.4
Central Plain	55.4	54.6	54.3
Bangkok	100.0	100.0	100.0

Source: Thailand, NESDB: Evaluation of the first half of the
         Fourth Plan (1977-78) (Bangkok, 1980), p. 6.

Table 3: Household income, expressed as a percentage of level
          in Bangkok, 1962-63 to 1975-76

Region	1962-63	1968-69	1975-76
North-east	31.7	29.3	43.8
North	32.0	31.6	44.0
South	50.4	33.6	52.7
Central Plain	52.1	48.2	65.7
Bangkok	100.0	100.0	100.0

Source: Adapted from IBRD: Income consumption and poverty in
         Thailand, 1962-63 to 1975-76, p. 20, and based on the
         household expenditure survey.

in table 2 on the other.   The two tables do not in fact measure
the same thing; one is household income, the other is GDP per
capita.   The differences between household sizes in the various
regions were small and would not affect comparison between the two
tables.   The gap between the two must then originate from two
sources.   First, there is the possible effect of remittances
earned by migrant workers and transferred back to the region of
origin.   These sums would figure in the estimates of income,
but not of regional GDP.   According to an official source, more
than one-third of the total household income of farmers was
derived from outside agriculture (see table 4).   Our data which
will be presented below also show that these remittances are
certainly large.   Secondly, there is the possibility of a steady
widening of the gap between the capital and these two upcountry
regions.

Table 4:   Average annual household income of farmers and their
            sources by region, 1969-76 (in baht)

Region	Total house-hold income (1)	Income from agriculture (2)	Income from other sources (3)	$\frac{(3)}{(1)}$%
North-east	6 661	3 310	3 351	50.3
North	10 663	7 434	3 229	30.9
South	11 592	4 499	6 093	52.6
Central Plain	18 247	13 149	5 098	27.9
Whole kingdom	10 903	6 588	4 315	39.6

Source: Ministry of Agriculture, cited in Supachai Panitchpakdi,
           "Employment effects of Tambol development programme: a
           note", paper presented at the Rural Employment Programmes
           and Local Level Planning for the Satisfaction of Basic
           Needs in Thailand with Special Emphasis on the Experiences
           and Lessons of the Tambol Development Programme, 1975-76,
           by ILO-ARTEP, 28-29 June 1976, Bangkok.

The North-east is notorious for its poverty. Moreover, the
region is not just a small backwater. It covers about one-third
of the kingdom and includes about one-third of the population.
The density of population in the North-east is higher than in the
other two outlying regions, though below that in the Central Plain.
In the other regions, and especially in the Central Plain, the
growth of population since the Second World War has been associated
with a growth of tenancy, and the causal mechanism has clearly
been the increasing pressure of population on land and thus the
emergence of a Ricardian rent. In 1976, the rate of tenancy
among agricultural households was reckoned to be 41 per cent in
the Central Plain, 27 per cent in the North and 17 per cent in
the South. In the North-east, however, despite the comparatively
heavy pressure of population, fewer than 9 per cent of households
took land on lease.[24] The reason for this discrepancy, and
indeed the key to the problem of the North-east's poverty, is the
abysmal quality of most of the region's agricultural land. The
region has few major rivers, and these are subject to flooding.
Most of the land depends on rainfall for the water necessary for
cultivation, and while it gets as much rainfall as other parts of
the country, the temperature is very high and the soil very
porous, with the result that the efficiency of rainfall is very
low. The porosity of the soil also defeats efforts to store
rainwater in irrigation tanks, while the existence of sub-soil
saline deposits has frustrated most of the efforts to develop
irrigation by wells. Drought is therefore common. The yield
of paddy is lower than in other regions of the country. In such
unattractive natural conditions, the ratio of labour input to final
agricultural product is very high; it takes a lot of care and
work to get any sort of yield at all. The individual peasant
family is hard-pressed to derive a subsistence income. There is
no margin for rent. Tenancy rates and per capita income are thus
both very low.

In the past two decades, the infrastructure of the region
improved enormously, principally through the construction of good
roads to the United States airforce bases in the region.[25] The
result has been a considerable expansion of acreage, and the
extension of new crops (cassava, sugar, maize) which can be grown
for a commercial market rather than local consumption. But
expansion has not done much to dent the level of poverty.

Working on such poor land with traditional methods, the farming
family cannot do much to raise its income above subsistence level,
whatever the crop that is being grown.   The difficulty faced by
the farmers of the North-east, as the Thai economic planners are
now beginning to recognise, is a shortage of the capital that is
necessary to introduce technology which will raise the productivity
of labour.[26]   At the moment the statistical expansion of production in the North-east merely means that the region is slowly
filling up, under the impetus of demographic increase, with more
and more farmers of a roughly similar level of desperate poverty.

The case of the North is rather different.   Along the rivers
there are tracts of good alluvial land which produce some of the
best rice yields in the whole country.   But outside these narrow
tracts, farming is again poor.   The land is often situated on
a hillside, and irrigation is difficult.   Moreover, within
villages in the North, poverty is often the result of the uneven
distribution of resources.   In one village studied in 1971-72,
a third of all families had no land, about a half had less than
one acre, and almost three-quarters had less than the two acres
which constituted the irreducible minimum for family subsistence.[27]
The vast majority of families thus depended on tenancy and wage
labour.   Even with renting, less than half the families could
gain access to enough land to support themselves, and the remainder
were forced to accept a humiliating indenture on the farm of a
more successful relative, or shuttle between the village and the
town in search of all sorts of casual and seasonal jobs.[28]

A comparative study of three villages in the same region
was undertaken from 1969 under a project in which the ILO had a
guiding role.[29]   One of the three villages was strongly under
the influence of a nearby town, and showed a skewed distribution
of land.   A third of the families had no land, another half
survived by renting in land, and only a sixth farmed entirely
owned land.   In the villages which were more remote from the
town, the distribution of land was significantly more even.
Most of the families owned some land and only 15 to 18 per cent
was rented.   In these latter villages, however, average incomes
were much lower.   This was mainly the result of a lack of
alternative employment and the prevalence of backward and inefficient techniques.   These latter characteristics can be seen as
evidence of the other factor which makes the North comparatively

poor - that is, its remoteness and the poor development of
communications.   The North is relatively far away from the hub of
economic activity in Bangkok, and lies at the bottom of a kind of
cul-de-sac - the trade over the hill ranges, besides the rather
specialised business of opium, is rather small.   Unlike the North-
east, the North was not opened up by good new roads in the 1960s.
There is only a scant network of reasonable roads, and away from
these the routes soon deteriorate into bumpy tracks.

The World Bank's survey of income and poverty in Thailand,
based on the 1975-76 household survey, found that the per capita
income of farmers in the North-east and North was 188 and 240 baht
per month respectively, and that of farm and general workers was
208 and 206 baht.   These figures compare with an average for the
whole kingdom of 324, and an average for Bangkok (or at least,
as noted above, for a Bangkok with a large rural appendix) of 605.[30]
Moreover, the World Bank survey reckoned that 31 per cent of the
Thai population lived below a poverty line calculated according
to an international standard, and that the vast majority of them
were in the North and North-east.   Of the total number of
Thailand's poor, 49 per cent were living in the villages of the
North-East, and another 22 per cent in the villages of the North.[31]
To put it the other way round, a third of the rural population of
the North, and nearly half the rural population of the North-east,
fell below the poverty line.

x x x x

Many of the inhabitants of the North and North-east clearly
felt that the only way to avoid such poverty was to run away.
The last census taken in 1970 found that the rate of migration
had increased by two-thirds since the previous count a decade
before, and that the North-east had "experienced the largest net
outflow of migrants (over 42,000 in 1965-70)".[32]

Most of the migration recorded in the 1970 census was either
short-distance movements within the major cities and their
immediate environs (especially Bangkok), or local shifts between
two relatively close rural regions, usually connected with marriage.
The latter was particularly common in the Central Plain which,
as noted above, has a very mobile population.   Yet there were

also clear patterns in the movement between regions. Tables 5,
6 and 7 show lifetime migrations (a shift of residence since birth)
and migrations in the period 1965-70, which took place across
regional boundaries. The tables show the high volume of migration
out of the North and North-east regions, destined for Bangkok and
for the Central Plain; because of the narrow definition of Bangkok
in this census, many of the suburbs and satellite towns of the
capital were counted in the Central Plain. More important than
volume, however, is the evidence on sex ratios. The authors of
the census noted that one of the most striking changes between
the data on migration in 1960 and that in 1970 concerned the
proportion between men and women. Migration streams are often
dominated by men, and Thailand (where traditionally the men rather
than the women shift home at marriage) is no exception.

Table 5: Lifetime migration between regions, 1970 census
(All figures in 000s. Each entry: Male)
Female

Region of birth From	Region of residence in 1970				
	North-east	North	Central Plain	Bangkok	South
North-east		723 548	646 393	550 658	219 87
North	229 201		267 270	324 450	42 63
Central Plain	535 266	980 915		2 186 2 288	342 276
Bangkok	139 133	112 99	593 508		111 104
South	38 38	37 30	95 95	289 258	

Source: Thailand, National Statistical Office: 1970 population
and housing census, subject report no. 2: Migration
by Fred Arnold and Supani Boonpratuang (Bangkok, 1978),
tables 6 and 9, pp. 41-42 and 46-47.

Table 6: <u>Migration between regions 1965-70, 1970 census</u>
(All figures in 000s. Each entry: Male)
                                     Female

| Region of origin | Region of residence in 1970 | | | | |
From	North-east	North	Central Plain	Bangkok	South
North-east		201	266	228	86
		142	208	310	34
North	220		142	125	9
	205		157	158	12
Central Plain	177	267			
	147	241			
Bangkok	118	70			
	90	56			
South	24	11	52	134	
	18	8	51	117	

Source: Thailand, National Statistical Office: <u>1970 population
and housing census</u>, subject report no. 2: <u>Migration</u> by
Fred Arnold and Supani Boonpratuang (Bangkok, 1978),
tables 6 and 9, pp. 41-42 and 46-47.

Table 7: <u>Migration into Bangkok 1965-70, by age and sex</u>

Age groups	Male (000s)	Female (000s)
5-9	143	130
10-14	168	199
15-19	360	448
20-24	461	344
25-29	199	196
Other	389	404
Total	1 720	1 721

Source: Thailand, National Statistical Office: <u>1970 population
and housing census</u>, subject report no. 2: <u>Migration</u>,
table 10, pp. 48-49. Based on sample data.

But between the 1960 and 1970 counts, the ratio of men to women in
the migration of the preceding five years fell from 131 : 100 to
115 : 100.   Tables 5 and 6 show that female migration was significantly stronger between certain regions.   In the migrations of
1965-70 men exceeded women in all but three inter-regional streams:
from the North-east to Bangkok, and from the North to both Bangkok
and the Central Plain.   In the movement from the North-east to
Bangkok, women exceeded men in the ratio of roughly 4 : 3, and in
the movement from the North to Bangkok by 5 : 4.   A similar
pattern occurs in the table of lifetime migration.   Table 6 shows
the age distribution of the 1965-70 migrants into Bangkok.
Unfortunately the data are slightly confused because they include
movements between the two districts (jangwats) which comprise
the city.   Still they show that the migrants were most concen-
trated in the age range from 15 to 24, and that it is in the
range from 10 to 19 that the women exceed the men.   Noting the
flow of women from the North and North-east, the census narrator
blandly commented: "Evidently Bangkok offers attractive opportunities for women from these regions".[33]

Migration into Bangkok has almost certainly increased in
the 1970s.   Table 7 extracts data from the 1978 labour force
survey.   It is dangerous to compare this too rigorously with
the census material, largely because the survey does not disclose
its definition of a migrant.   Probably, however, it refers to
a migrant within the last five years.   If that is so, the data
show large increases in migration in the 1970s, particularly from
the North-east.   Women still outnumber men in the movement from
the North to the city, although the ratios in the flow from the
North-east have been reversed.   (Women exceed men in the flow
from the Central Plain also, but this may be misleading.   The
data show that Central Plain migrants came mainly from the towns,
and thus may include many short-distance movements within the
conurbation of Bangkok.   Most of the North and North-east
migrants originated in the countryside.)   The final column of
the table, moreover, shows that while on average only 44.4 per
cent of the city's women (over 11 years) participate in the labour
force, the rate of participation by migrant women from the North
is 54.5 per cent, and among migrant women from the North-east it
soars up to 80.8 per cent.   If we eliminate students from the
calculations of labour participation rates, the average for the

city women comes to 56.3 per cent, while for the North migrants
it is 67.4 per cent, and for the North-east migrants it is
85.2 per cent.

⁕ ⁕ ⁕ ⁕

Table 8: Migrants in Bangkok, 1978

	Male (000s)	Female (000s)	Female participation in labour force Percentage
Total population	13 643	14 320	44.4
Non-migrants	11 930	12 585	41.6
From North-east	886	817	80.8
From North	173	238	54.5
From Central Plain	474	531	55.5
From South	153	127	27.0

Source: Thailand, National Statistical Office: Report of the
labour force survey, 1978, table 5.

The two poorest regions of the country thus export large
numbers of migrants to the richer regions, and particularly to
the metropolis of Bangkok. In these streams of migrants, there
are as many women as men, if not more. The women come not just
as adjuncts to their menfolk, but as workers in their own right.
The prominent part women from the North and North-east play both
in the migration stream and in the labour force at the other end
reflects the economic and social dimensions of their position in
the village.

Within these streams of migrants there are many young girls
who will finish up in the bars and massage parlours of Bangkok.
The exact orientation of the two different regions to this trade
is rather different. The North-east was introduced to the
business through the foreign bases located in the region during

the Viet Nam war.   Many girls recruited locally in this way
later made their way to the brighter lights of Bangkok, and after
the bases were closed the focus clearly shifted to the capital.
The migration of these girls, however, formed only a minor part
of a larger migration from the North-east which was driven along
by the harsh facts of economic necessity.   The factories and
service industries of the city are staffed with a high proportion
of workers (of both sexes) who have fled from the barren soils
and seemingly inevitable poverty of the North-east.   The girls
are not reckoned to have any special advantage in the night-life
trade.   Characteristically they are not especially pretty or
sophisticated.   Their involvement in the trade is the combined
result of comparative economic opportunities and the Viet Nam war.
From the North, by contrast, the economic imperative is not quite
as pressing, and indeed the over-all size of the migration stream
is much lower than from the North-east.   The Northern girls,
however, are reckoned to have considerable advantages in the
massage business.   They are considered pretty and charming by
nature.   If it was the Viet Nam war which drew in the North-east
girls, it was the institution of the beauty contest which provided
the channel for the girls from the North.

The villages

We traced girls back to five different villages - one in
the North-east and four in the North.   The villages are listed
below and shown on the map overleaf.

Area	Village	Amphoe	Province
North-east	Don Barg	Phen	Udon
North	Tung Kwian	Mae Eye	Chiengmai
North	San Pa Daeng	Vieng Pa Pao	Chiengmai
North	Sri Chum	Dok Kam Tai	Payao
North	San Ton Mue	Phang	Chiengmai

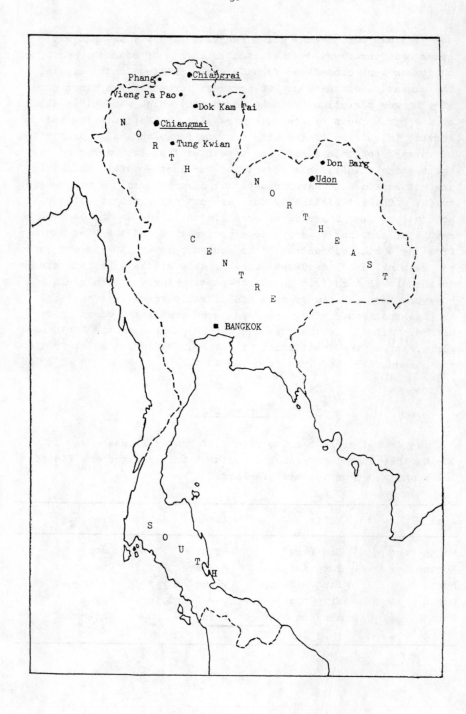

In each village we spent some time gathering data from local officials, and getting information on attitudes towards the migration of girls by talking at random with men and women in the village. In addition we conducted 13 extended interviews, five with returned migrants and eight with the families of migrants.

The villages were very much alike in having poor agriculture and low living standards, but the particular characteristics of their poverty showed interesting differences. We have divided the villages into three separate groups, and will begin with the North-eastern village.

Don Barg, Udon Province: Missing out on development

Don Barg is remote. It is 60 kms away from the provincial capital of Udon, which in turn is 510 kms away from Bangkok. The distance of the village away from Udon is magnified by the relatively poor state of communications. A regular bus runs from Udon along a good paved road to the Amphoe town of Phen. From there, however, the last 20 kms are on gravel roads. There is a bus but it runs only twice a day, and the alternative is to pay a phenomenal fee[34] for a motorised tricycle powered by a scooter engine which bumps along through a series of similar-looking rice-growing villages until it discovers Don Barg screened off behind rows of bamboos.

The village has 102 households and about 1,200 acres, 1,040 of which are planted with rice. Most of the households own some land and only five families are completely landless. The largest holding was 56 acres, and the smallest 4.8, with the average around 10 acres per household. These figures are high by Thai standards, but the reason is the poor quality of the soil not the prosperity of the villagers. The soil is heavy and low in nutrient. It gets baked hard by the sun and is difficult to work both in the hot season and during the rains. And hard work gets poor rewards. The average yield of paddy per acre (as reported by villagers in local units and converted into metric) was 938 kgs in a good year and 750 kgs in a bad year. On the very bad soils of the village, the yield could drop down as low as 62.5 kgs per year. On average, the income per person/month from growing paddy (including that

part retained for household consumption) would be about 8 baht
in a bad year.   The World Bank's estimate of the poverty level
for rural Thailand was 7.5 baht in 1975-76,[35] and the figure
would be nearer 10 baht in 1980.   Despite the obvious crudity of
calculations like this, it is clear that agriculture in Don Barg,
even on pretty well-sized holdings, can hardly keep a family
above subsistence.

The local economy has hardly been affected by the changes
that have overtaken the region since the early 1960s.   The
provincial town of Udon used to be a sleepy town on the route
from Bangkok to Laos, but in the 1960s it was jerked into the
modern world when the United States built an airbase just outside
the town, and subsequently built a gleaming new highway to link
Udon to Bangkok.   Udon mushroomed into a thriving service town.
By the time the Americans left, it had become well enough established as a marketing centre that it survived and continued to pros-
per.   The improvement in communications had encouraged the farmers
in the surrounding area to plant new crops of jute and maize destined
for export.   Udon became a major marketing centre for these new products.   Then in the late 1970s, Udon again felt the effect of the
Indochina conflict when it became a headquarters of the UNHCR's pro-
grammes to provide for the refugees along Thailand's fraught borders.

Some of the young men from Don Barg went to work in Udon
during the 1960s' boom, but the wage rates are now low (about 15
to 25 baht a day) and although some of the young villagers still
go, it does not result in much flow of cash back into the village.
Nor did Don Barg feel the effects of the new roads.   Villages
and farms sited along the course of the new highway felt the
effects of the reduction in transport costs and responded eagerly
to the stimulus to grow new crops.   But the poor state of local
communications meant that the cost advantages of the new road
declined steeply for villages which were any distance from the
highway.   Don Barg grows no maize, jute or cassava at all.

The village continues to use old and inefficient techniques.
It grows rice, mainly for subsistence, using buffalo for draught
power and relying on the rain for moisture.   The villagers
also continue to supplement their meagre agricultural income by
traditional methods.   The married women still weave their own
cloth, make their own bedding, and fashion their own household
utensils.   They catch fish in the village pond, and they weave

baskets for home use and for sale in the local markets. But even
traditional sources of extra income are coming under threat.
One of the major resources of Don Barg used to be the forest area
around the outskirts of the village. Many of the villagers,
despite their evident poverty, live in large, old wooden houses
which were clearly built at a time when timber was cheap and
easily available. Don Barg villagers used also to build wooden
houses for sale (the business of CKD* traditional wooden houses
is quite common in Thailand). But now the tracts around the
village contain only some bamboo clumps, and some traces of old
tree stumps. There are no new houses in the village. And there
is no sign of the house construction trade.

Phang and Dok Kam Tai:
Dry-farming and drugs

Like Don Barg, the two Northern Amphoe of Phang and Dok Kam Tai
are distant and remote. Also like Don Barg, they show clear signs
that the margin of forest lands has been rapidly eroded with painful results for the local economy. But while it is unlikely
that Don Barg was ever a wealthy place, Phang and Dok Kam Tai
have some clear signs of past prosperity.

Dok Kam Tai, for instance, is an Amphoe of about 60 villages
in the low-lying hills which surround the Northern provincial
capital of Chiengmai. The distance from Bangkok is about 550 kms
and the last stretches are along windy roads across the hill
ranges. The village which we visited, Sri Chum, has a number
of large and beautiful old teak houses. These are not simply
the product of good local supplies of wood, as in Don Barg, but
also the fruits of conspicuous consumption on the part of men
of commerce. The area lay across one of the trading routes across
the hills, and later had a role in the rich opium trade.

---

* CKD = completely knocked down, as in CKD parts of automobiles
and furniture. The wooden houses are built, sold, dismantled
and transported for reassembling on the purchaser's plot. This
practice is adopted to get around laws inhibiting the transport
of unworked timber across regions.

Trading opportunities have since diminished and the area has been forced back towards agriculture.   Paddy is grown on the flatter areas among the hills, using mainly rainfall for irrigation with some occasional supplement from mountain streams. In the areas where there is an assured supply of water all the year round, the farmers grow small amounts of peanuts, mushrooms, maize, tobacco and garlic.   But such areas are quite limited, and most of the land has to lie unused during the dry season.

Meanwhile, the average size of holding is very small.   In the whole Amphoe, there are about 60,000 people and about 35,000 cultivated acres.   Five families have holdings over 100 acres, and another 120 have holdings between 25 and 100 acres. Most of these larger holdings have been rented out, and the holders become absentee landlords living in the nearby towns. The remaining 9,000 holdings average out a little over three acres apiece.   Two thousand families, meanwhile, own no land at all.   Local opinion estimated that two to three acres is the minimum necessary for family subsistence (provided that it is reasonably good land), while six to seven acres is required to ensure an income sufficient to cover basic cash expenses.   The proceeds of agriculture, therefore, are barely enough to keep the majority of families safely above the subsistence line.   For those who own no land at all, there is either the chance of renting land, usually for a two-thirds crop share, or the precarious business of picking up wage work on the larger farms.

Finally, the farmers of these Northern areas have an additional problem which is a direct consequence of the remoteness of the villages.   They are situated at the very end of chains of rural marketing, and thus they not only get poor prices for their products, but suffer particularly badly from the swings of demand. When demand for a certain crop begins to drop, it is the furthest tips of the marketing system which begin to wither first. Farmers in these areas complained that even when they took the risks of investing in new and commercial crops, they all too often found that the market was unreliable and the produce was difficult to sell.

But if that is the picture for the entire Amphoe, the situation in the village of Sri Chum is noticeably worse.   Sri Chum is known for the poor quality of the soil and the difficult state of irrigation. The soil is clay, and the irrigation sources almost non-existent. The majority of farmers try to scrape up a living by making straw hats and pottery for sale, or by collecting forest products and taking them to market. A few also make a reasonable income by selling silkworms.

The Amphoe of Phang further to the north and even more remote, is not significantly different from Dok Kam Tai. There is the same story of limited supplies of land and very limited resources of irrigation. There is a river running through the Amphoe, and one or two prosperous farms which can use its water. But the steepness of the valley slopes means that irrigation works cannot be extended far from the river without some considerable difficulty. Rain-fed agriculture must adhere to a strict seasonal rhythm, and the combination of poverty, a long off-season and an age-old association with the opium traffic has contributed to special problems in both Phang and Dok Kam Tai. In both Amphoes there are very high rates of crime among young people. One survey in Dok Kam Tai reckoned that almost a third of the teenagers, who had little to do for a large part of the agricultural year, were addicted to opium.[36] The daily cost of a fix usually starts at around 10 baht, but quickly rises to 20, and impels the addict to find the money by criminal methods, if necessary. The Public Prosecutor of Dok Kam Tai noted that the incidence of addiction was inversely related to the provision of water in the villages, with the parched hamlet of Sri Chum being especially notorious for the number of its addicts and its robberies. The authorities have enormous difficulty in suppressing the opium trade since it is run by powerful local notables.

Until the early 1970s it was difficult for the children in these villages to get more than four years of primary education at the local school. Since then, the provision of better roads and the construction of rural secondary schools has put more education within the reach of the village children, and the rate of enrolment has increased rapidly. The Government has also made attempts to increase the opportunities for non-agricultural employment, but so far these have been somewhat limp. An occupational training centre in Dok Kam Tai provides girls with the chances of training in lines like cookery and dressmaking. At the moment, however, migration still provides by far the best opportunities. As we shall see below, the girls of Phang and Dok Kam Tai, especially the village of Sri Chum, have acquired a special notoriety.

Vieng Pa Pao and Tung Kwian: Invasion of the city people

Vieng Pa Pao and Tung Kwian are in the North, but they are nowhere near as remote as Phang and Dok Kam Tai. Vieng Pa Pao lies across the road which leads out of the regional capital of Chiengmai towards the North, while Tung Kwian straddles the road from Chiengmai to the South. Here the problems are a result both of the villages' basic poverty and of their collision with the forces of urban expansion.

Tung Kwian has 210 households and only 160 acres of land. The land is good and even the smallest holding of 1.6 acres yields enough rice to feed a family of six.[37] Moreover, it is reasonably evenly distributed among those who own land, and the largest holding is only eight acres. Those who own land also grow sugar cane for sale. But the vast majority of families - over three-quarters of the total - had no land at all. There was no obvious explanation proffered locally for this extreme imbalance. The villagers merely said that the place had always been poor. Some of the landless seek work on the farms in the village, but the demand is not enough to support all of them. Others go off to work in the nearby towns, or in the forest reserves close by. Meanwhile the middle-aged and older women gather forest products such as bamboo shoots, wild mushrooms, other vegetables, squirrels and edible toads. Some of this produce is sold along the roadside. Other families engaged in charcoal making. They cut the tress in the forest areas around the village and sold the charcoal in the urban markets nearby.

For the landless villagers of Tung Kwian, the forests provided an immensely important resource. As in Don Barg, there were many large wooden houses in the village which were now inhabited by quite poor families and which clearly had been built with wood which was easily available and cheap. Meanwhile, the forest also provided a source of food and of saleable products, and even crated employment in the government reserves. Recent developments in the control of the forest, however, had presented the landless villagers with serious problems.

In the early 1970s, the landless villagers, with the support
of some students, petitioned the Ministry of Interior for permission
to open up a portion of the forest reserve for farming.[*]   After
a considerable agitation, permission was finally granted, but
the villagers did not get the benefit.   When they tried to occupy
the land, the local officials announced that there were still some
outstanding problems about the legal documentation and dissuaded
them from taking up the land for the moment.   Matters dragged on
and the villagers voiced their impatience, but then the local
police were mobilised to threaten the villagers with dire consequences should they take matters into their own hands.   After
considerable provocation, the villagers were persuaded to give
up their demand for the land.   Soon after, the tract was given
over to an army officer who seemed to have much less difficulty
with the legal paraphernalia.   He turned the tract into a pine-
apple plantation.   Virtually all of the young people from the
landless families of the village now migrate to Chiengmai and
other cities for work.

Vieng Pa Pao is also a poor village with no large houses,
and a considerable crime problem.   The police establishment in
the place is out of all proportion to the village's size.   There
have been attempts among the villagers to start fish farms, to
cultivate mushrooms, and to grow fermented tea (myang) on the
hill slopes.   But most depend on low-level agriculture.   Until
recently there was another sideline which provided the villagers
with some income.   The surrounding area is rich in deposits of
tin, many of which are very easily accessible.   There was a
mine, owned by a small local company, which not only provided
some work for the villagers, but also purchased ores which the
villagers collected themselves.   The men of the village often
worked small diggings, or dredged in the streams, and could get
a reasonable income from it.   Subsequently a large mining company
took over the mine, and established a mining concession which
extended over the whole area around the village.   They have not

---

[*] The following historical account is based on interviews
with villagers who were involved in the dispute.

only ceased purchasing the villagers' gleanings, but have banned
all small-scale mining and dredging in their concession territory.
When villagers tried to evade this ban, the company used the local
police to prevent them.

Thus in both Tung Kwian and Vieng Pa Pao new urban investment
has blocked off the opportunities available to the villagers who
do not have adequate access to land.

* * * *

Several themes run through these descriptions of different
villages. First, within the relatively backward areas of the
North and North-east, these were among the less well-endowed or
more remote of the villages. Second, in the past these villages
had relied heavily on non-agricultural sources of income, particularly from the forest or marginal areas around the village.
The depletion or annexation of these resources had created a
particularly difficult situation for the landless families. Third,
there were few opportunities for local employment. In those
villages where the agricultural cycle included a long-off season,
this tended to force many of the young people into a choice between
enforced idleness with the temptation to crime, or migration.

Don Barg in the North-east and Tung Kwian in the North sent
very few girls as migrants. Vieng Pa Pao, Phang and Dok Kam Tai,
however, were heavily involved. From Vieng Pa Pao, girls had
started going to work as maids in the towns and cities, and several
of them had gradually drifted into the area of "special services".
The migration from the precarious rain-fed villages in the North
had got going in the early 1970s when a sustained series of years
of poor rainfall created a considerable local crisis. Since then
Dok Kam Tai in particular had gained a considerable notoriety
for the number of girls who "went South". The girls were renowned
not only for their number but also for their beauty, and a
Dok Kam Tai girl commanded a small premium in the trade. Several
girls in the village who had "been South" and returned had subsequently set themselves up as agents who provided "guaranteed
Dok Kam Tai" girls to certain places in Bangkok. The postmaster
of the Amphoe estimated that the level of postal remittances to
the village had multiplied 130 times in the six years in which
he had held the post. In 1979, the total of remittances by

postal order into Dok Kam Tai had totalled ฿76 million (estimated
for the researchers by the postmaster, whose account book was also
consulted).   This created considerable problems since the postal
organisation, basing its estimates on the usual usage, provided
the postmaster with an annual drawing capacity of only ฿3.6 million to clear postal orders.

The local attitude towards the girls who "went South" was
rather mixed.   In the North-east, the attitude appeared to be
definitely more strict.   Pre-marital sex and promiscuity were
definitely frowned upon.   In the village we studied, the village
headman did not accept that certain female members of his village
had gone to work in the town of Udon as temporary wives of
foreigners during the 1960s.   Yet we found two women who said
they had worked as temporary wives.   The wife of the village
headman showed a scornful look when we asked for the direction of
the house of the girl who had gone South.   She did not say
anything, but it was more than obvious that she did not wish to
associate herself with that household.   We asked the girls who
had been South about the attitudes of the villagers towards them.
They said that the villagers had been very understanding.   They
might say things behind their backs but they had never done anything
which offended them.   Three of the girls who had been South had
returned and married men outside the village.   They all lived
at their husband's village.   When we asked the men in Don Barg
about their attitude towards girls who had gone South, they said
that no one around the village would marry these girls.   When we
asked the reasons, it appeared that it was because the men felt
that the girls had become too sophisticated and too accustomed to
urban life and luxuries, such that the village men would find it
difficult to match or control them.   They did not really dislike
these girls and were not contemptuous of them.   They just felt
that the girls had become so different that it would be difficult
to get on.   The older women, however, thought that the girls who
went South had done improper things.   They did not wish to
associate themselves and remained rather aloof.

In the North, the mixture of sympathy and distaste was even
more complex.   Fundamental views about sex and about marital
relations were rather more relaxed than in the North-east, as is
clear from an anthropological study in the Chiengmai area in the
early 1970s:

"There are very few separated or divorced wives in the three villages. Divorce does not have any social stigma among the villagers. Women who are divorced have their own independent lives without incurring gossip from the villagers. Remarriage is not a scandalous matter. The woman can have children by her new husband, and the children who are born from the former and the new marriage can live with the new husband who helps to provide for the children's education."[38]

But any amount of liberal predisposition could not cope with the kind of notoriety which places like Dok Kam Tai acquired in the space of a decade. A village headman and deputy district officer who spoke frankly to a newspaper about the depth of the village's involvement in the flesh trade were forced to resign after an angry demonstration by local inhabitants. The rural development officer at the provincial headquarters denied flatly that there was anything special about Dok Kam Tai. Others were more sympathetic and realistic. The village headman in Phang admitted that about half of the young girls in the village were involved in the business and that it had become self-sustaining. Girls who returned from the South with money and a touch of glamour provided a model which their younger counterparts were anxious to follow. He blamed the matter on the poor opportunities for local employment.

In general in the North, people's attitude differed depending on the social classes. The middle-class, well-educated people looked down upon the masseuses and the girls who went South. But the poorer villagers' attitude was much more relaxed. However, it is difficult to generalise because the attitude varies from village to village. In the four villages studied, we had the impression that the villagers attached no real social stigma to the girls who went South, although girls who came back as "failures" felt that they were sneered at by other villages. But they did not care very much. As to the question whether going South would have obstructed their marriage prospects, the answer was generally negative. The men's attitude was also interesting. Two of the young men interviewed said that they would not mind marrying girls who had gone South, and were sympathetic towards their reasons for going. As to the question of whether they would mind if after the marriage the girls went South again, they replied that they would not mind if the girls went because of real economic reasons. In other words, if they both could not earn enough to feed the family and there was only

one way out, the girl might have to go back to her old trade.
But they would mind terribly if their wives took lovers for
personal reasons.   They said they would not stand that and would
want a divorce.   Parents interviewed thought that girls who went
South were better than before because they had become prettier
and richer.   When asked if they would like their son to marry
one of the girls who had gone South, the answer was no.   There
appeared to be some kind of double standard.   We interviewed one
woman who returned to her village and was then married to a low-
rank policeman.   She said she had no problems adjusting herself
back to the village life and did not feel that she was discriminated
against by the villagers.   To her, marrying a policeman was a
step up in the world.   She felt she had done well for herself.
She would like her daughter to be a teacher and was determined to
send her to a good school.

Several people in the North stressed that they admired the
girls for the loyalty which they showed towards their parents.
They appreciated that the girls were not running away, but rather
were showing a proper filial responsibility for looking after their
parents in old age.   They were sympathetic to the economic con-
straints which operated within such poor regions and within such
poor villages, and were prepared to see it as an economic rather
than a moral issue.   To examine the dimensions of that loyalty
in greater detail, we must now look at the case histories of a
few of the girls themselves.

The girls[*]

Taew
(from Don Barg, Udon, in the North-east)

Taew is the third child of a family of eight.   She was 21
when we met her, and had two elder sisters of 23 and 25.   A younger
sister of 17 was in secondary school and another of 13 still in
elementary school along with two brothers aged six and nine.
Taew and her two elder sisters had managed to acquire only four
years of elementary schooling apiece.   Taew was obviously
the prettiest one of the family.   She was lightly built, quite
fair, and had unusually beautiful hands and feet for a farmer's

---

[*] All the personal names are fictitious.

daughter.   She looked frail, and had a pretty but sad face which immediately invited sympathy.

Taew's father was a Laotian who had come to work in Thailand as a wage labourer.   He had met his wife while working in Khon Khaen, a major town in the North-east about 100 kms from Udon.   She came from a four-acre farming family and was one of four children.   When her father died, the land seemed too small to subdivide according to the usual custom, so it was sold to the eldest daughter.   Taew was born in Khon Khaen, and soon after the family, along with Taew's mother's younger sister, moved to Don Barg where Taew's father's brother had already settled. They thus arrived in this rather poor village as landless outsiders.

When Taew's family arrived in Dong Barg village over 20 years ago, they built a little thatched hut on the spare land adjacent to her father's brother's house.   They did not have to pay any rent, being very poor.   They helped the brother work on his land during the harvest season.   Taew's mother collected forest products to supplement the family's subsistence need.   The village was too far from the Amphoe to do any trading.   The sister of Taew's mother, Taew's aunt, went off to work as a housemaid in the town of Udon.   She earned enough cash to send a small sum back home.   When the United States built the air base, and Udon town was flooded with GIs, Taew's aunt lived with an officer, looked after his house and bore him a child.   They planned to get married, but he was killed in Viet Nam after the baby was born. Thus this aunt was left with this half-Thai daughter who was 12 years old at the time of our visit.

Taew's family struggled on in Don Barg, and every other year a new member of the family arrived.   Taew recalled that when she was small, the hut they lived in had several holes in the roof and they had to sleep in the downpour during the rainy season. Life in a remote village with no prospects for trading or wage labouring outside the agricultural season was very difficult for a landless family.   Driven by poverty, Taew's two elder sisters agreed to go to work in Udon.   Their aunt encouraged them.   They worked as mistresses to a group of GIs.   They cooked for them, looked after their house, and catered for their personal needs.   They earned quite well, and in the first year managed to send home ฿20,000 to build a new house for their parents.

In the second year, one of the sisters built a second house which
was later sold for cash.   In the third year, they bought the
parents 15 acres of rice land on the outskirts of the village.
They also managed to send their other brothers and sisters to
school.   The family's income had improved enormously, and things
went well until 1975, when the GIs left.   The sisters came back
to the village, lived off their past savings, and helped to farm
the land which they had bought.   But the soil was very poor.
In good years the yield was enough to provide for the family's
subsistence and have some rice left over to sell for cash to buy
other things.   But in a bad year, the return was reduced to
almost nothing.   The family had to borrow money, and go in search
of forest products to live on.   They also made charcoal to sell
in the nearby town, but wood was already getting scarce in the
vicinity and eventually this sideline collapsed.   One of the
sisters moved off to Bangkok to work as a masseuse, and has
remained there ever since.   The other followed suit soon after,
but did not like Bangkok and subsequently went off with the aunt
to Pattaya (a seaside resort) to work in a bar-cum-restaurant for
฿400 a month.   They got a bonus if they could persuade the
customers to order more drinks, and they were encouraged to earn
extra by sleeping with the customers.   Both the aunt and the
sister met their present husbands while working in Pattaya.
Both were from the North-east, though not from Don Barg, and both
were younger than their brides.   After the marriages, both the
women decided to quit Pattaya and return to the North-east to live
on their husbands' farms.   They now have a child each and during
our visit were staying in Don Barg to convalesce after childbirth.

When Taew's sister and aunt stopped working, the family lost
a good source of income.   Taew was then 18.   She was old enough
to work and was encouraged to go to live with the sister who
remained in Bangkok.   With only four years of elementary education behind her, Taew did not have much choice as far as work was
concerned.   However, she was naturally rather shy and did not
go straight to the massage parlour.   Her first job was on a construction site in Bangkok, where she mixed cement and tied steel
rods to make concrete columns.   It was not a very difficult task
but she had to work outside in the sun all day and got only
35 baht per day.   She lasted for a month on this job and then
moved to work as a housemaid in the household of the manager of

the construction company. For this job she got 400 baht a month, with food provided by the household. She worked here for four months, got tired of it and left to work as a waitress in a restaurant. A girlfriend found her this new job. It was one of those places where the waitresses were supposed to encourage the customers to drink by talking to them and making up to them. The girls got a commission of 5 baht for every glass of drinks the customer ordered. A good-looking and talkative girl would earn quite a bit of money in this way, particularly if she was prepared to have sexual relations with the customer. But Taew was very shy. She could earn only 20-30 baht a day. After working in this new place for a month, she found out that the owner of the restaurant made a lot of money from sending girls abroad to work as prostitutes. She was greatly alarmed and left the restaurant to stay with a girlfriend who used to work in the same restaurant. While staying in this friend's house she met another North-eastern girl who worked in a massage parlour in the evening. She was hard up for money, and decided to follow her friend to work as a masseuse. Thus after trying various other jobs for six to seven months, Taew was finally lured into working as a masseuse.

When she started at the massage parlour, Taew was still a virgin. At first she gave only a regular massage and got 18 baht per customer. Eventually she was persuaded to sell her virginity. The client paid ฿8,000, of which Taew got ฿2,000. She sent the money home to build a well for drinking water. Taew did not like it a bit. She cried for several days afterwards, and had to see a doctor. After that she had sexual relations with her customers to earn money, but she remained choosey and said she had only three customers. The second time she got ฿800 for it, and the third time she met her present boyfriend who would like to keep her as his mistress. He persuaded her to leave the job, sent her to study dressmaking and rented her a small room to live in. But once she stopped working she did not have any money to send home and her parents kept sending letters asking for money. Her boyfriend, who was a divorced man with three children of his own, could not afford both to keep her and to help with her family's financial problem. Taew decided to go back to work. But this time she did not go back to the massage parlour because she did not want to work every day. She was told by some of her

friends that she could earn a few thousand in a few days if she
could find a foreigner, who wanted a girl companion for a few days
while he spent his holidays in Bangkok.   The way to find these
men was to dress nicely and go to sit in Grace Hotel on Sukumwit
Road in the evening.   That was what she did after having a big
row with her boyfriend over financial problems.   She would not
tell me how much she earned from each customer, but she said that
her monthly income was between 3,000-4,000 baht.   She did not
like the job.   She did not go and sit in this hotel very often.
She only went when she needed the money, and she regularly sent
to her parents between 500-1,000 baht a month.   Her parents
needed the money for their everyday living and for the school fees
of her brothers and sisters.   Sometimes the parents requested a
larger sum of money.   She had had about four months of training
as a seamstress or a dressmaker, but made no use of the skill.
She explained that she often thought of applying for a seamstress
job, but she had not got round to it.   Besides, she knew that
she would get less than 1,000 baht a month, and did not think
the salary was attractive.   She had worked as a salesgirl for a
few weeks after her boyfriend had got her the job.   But she could
not stand working with lots of people.   She said they looked down
on her when they found out that she used to work as a masseuse.
She also disliked travelling by bus during the rush hour.   She
said she was so used to using taxis.   She thought having to work
on her own was too much hard work.   As to her future plans, she
said she did not know.   She would not mind being adopted as a
minor wife to a nice and rich person.   She did not trust her
present boyfriend because he had double standards and he was
not generous.

Taew allowed me to visit her parents on the condition that
I would not tell them that she had been working as a masseuse
and as a coffee-shop girl.[39]   I visited her home twice, the first
time I met her elder sister, who was convalescing after the birth
of her first child.   The second time I met her aunt, again during
convalescence after the birth of her first son.   Taew had told her
parents that she was working in a restaurant as a waitress.   I
told her parents that I met Taew in a restaurant while I was
making a study of migrant girls, and had traced her back to her
home.   The parents were very pleased to be visited.   I was
surprised that the parents did not in fact know of the true

occupation of their daughter.   It was difficult to believe.
The elder sister and the aunt knew.   The neighbours also knew,
but they did not say that they did.   They just said that a girl
with low education as Taew would not earn enough money from being
a waitress to send home a large sum each month.   The parents had
spread the news that their daughter was living with her husband,
a nice man in Bangkok.   The villagers said that if that was
true, then why did they not come back home to marry.   The parents
were obviously very proud of their daughter, although they were
quite worried about her future since there was no definite news
of the marriage.   The second time I went to visit, the mother
was quite uneasy about the situation and preferred to talk about
her other daughters who were then studying in secondary school.
Taew had sent the money to support these sisters.   I learned
from the second visit that the family no longer farmed their land.
They decided to rent all their land out because the father's
health had deteriorated, and because he could not rely on the
family labour to work on the farm while the younger children had
to go to school, Taew was living in Bangkok, and the elder
daughter had moved house to live with her husband and family in
another province.   The rent they charged was one-third of the
yearly crops.

We worked out that the family was much better off than before
and had more regular income.   In terms of cash earned, they were
still on a par with other poor farmers, but they had a better
and more secure house to live in.   They also had a good source
of water to drink and to use in the household from the well their
daughter made.   They had become landowners renting out land to
other peasants, even though their land was of poor soil.   But
with a large family and with no productive source of income of
their own, the family per capita income was still near enough to
the poverty line.   We estimated their yearly income from various
sources as follows:

	Baht per year
Rent from land	4,500
Sales of ducks and chicken	2,000-3,000
Sales of cotton cloth weaved by the mother	300-400
Remittances from two daughters	8,000-9,000
Total family income/year	14,800-16,900
per capita income/month	176-200
Poverty line as defined by the World Bank for rural households/person/month	150

It was possible that the family underestimated their income in order to get some sympathy from us. But from my observations and from spending some time talking to them I do not think they lied to us. The family did not have many possessions in the household and they ate very simply. Their basic diet consisted of sticky rice and pickled wild bamboo shoots, with lots of chilies and fish sauce. They got some of their rice from their farm, but that was usually not enough and they had to buy some more from the market. They had to buy the fish sauce and chilies, but the bamboo shoots they could find in the woods. The family also saved by weaving their own cotton cloth, although the children's school uniforms had to be bought from the market. The only family possessions of durable goods were a small transistor radio and a sewing machine.

It can be seen from the figures above that the family's main source of income was the remittances from their daughters. One would expect that they would channel the money received to more productive use, e.g. improving the farm and investing in husbandry and much more. But one can also see that that was difficult, largely because they had a large family and had decided to devote a large slice of their cash income to the school fees of three children. In the long run, sending the children to higher education might become the most productive investment, but the waiting period was very long. The daughter then studying in the third year at high school was the family's next prospect as a cash earner. But she may not earn as much as her masseuse sisters. It would take another three years to finish secondary school.

If she worked straight away after finishing secondary school, she
would get 800-1,000 baht a month.   To earn much more she would
need more years of education.   It is not very certain that the
family could afford to send their children to higher education
beyond secondary school.   It would probably depend on whether
the two elder sisters would be willing to send more money.

Lek
(from Tung Kwian village, Amphoe
Mae Eye, Chiengmai Province, North)

The Family Profile:

Members of family	Age	Education	Occupation	Present place of work or residence
Father	51	P.4[1]	Farmer/wage labourer	Chiengmai
Mother	46	None	Farmer/wage labourer	Chiengmai
Children:				
1. Son	22	P.4[1]	Wage labourer	Provincial town
2. Daughter	16	Can read and write, not yet finished P.4[1]	Masseuse	Bangkok
3. Daughter	14	P.4[1]	Help around	Chiengmai
4. Daughter	10	None	-	Chiengmai
5. Son		None	-	Chiengmai

[1] Prathom 4 or 4th grade in elementary education

I first met Lek in a fifth-grade massage parlour which is
actually a whore-house.   The place is tucked away in a little
lane in Suriwong, the centre of the business world of Bangkok.
Lek worked as a "bonded girl" there.   The agent who brought Lek
to Bangkok had lent her parents 1,500 baht on the condition that
Lek came to work in Bangkok to pay off the debt.   She had arrived

a few weeks before I talked to her. She was plump and not at all
good-looking, but she had a smiling and friendly face. She still
had the look of a little girl and her figure was not fully developed.
She did not appear to be miserable, as she was smiling all the time
while we were talking. When asked if she liked the job, she said
she did not. She would like to go home. When asked when she
could go home, she said she did not know. Perhaps she would go
home when she paid off the debt. As to the question when did she
think she would work off the debt, the reply was she did not know.
She could free herself if she could repay the loan of 1,500 baht
by entertaining her customers. Since she got 10 baht per hour/
customer, she would have to entertain at least 150 customers or
work there 150 hours in order to work off her debts. However,
she said that only a week ago her parents had come to ask her
employer for an advance on her wage of another 1,500 baht. So
this means that she had to stay longer in this place before she
could be free, and she did not know when her freedom could be
regained.

Lek must have come from a very poor family, I thought.

When we visited her home, we were surprised to find that her
parents lived in a rather lovely old wooden house. It was not
large but rather well built in a nice compound with a small space
around it. It looked as if at one time the family was not that
poor. Lek's parents had inherited the house from their own
parents who died in the early 1960s. The grandparents had eight
acres of rice land, which was divided between their two children,
Lek's mother and Lek's uncle, just before the parents' death.
Lek's mother also inherited the family home because she looked
after the grandparents in their old age. With four acres of rice
land to work on, the family was self-sufficient in food at least,
and in good years they had surplus rice to sell for cash to buy
other things. But the family was never that rich. The grandparents' health was bad towards the end of their lives and a lot
of the cash earned had to be spent on medical bills. The family
had accumulated a rather large sum of debt by the time the grandparents passed away. Soon after the grandparents' death there
were successive years of bad rainfall. The family had to borrow
money continually to pay for their subsistence and for the cultivation of their rice crop, which never yielded a good income. The
eldest son went off to work as a tricycle driver in Chiengmai and

sent a little sum of money home once in a while. He soon got
married, started a family of his own, and stopped sending money
home. The bad rainfall lasted from 1966 to 1974. Initially,
they could borrow from their relatives, but as they borrowed
more and more their relatives could no longer help them. Having
failed to get help from relatives, the family had to borrow from
a merchant in town who demanded their land as collateral. Lek's
parents borrowed 5,000 baht using their land as a collateral under
the condition that they had to return the principal and the
interest within one year. If they failed to return the money
at the specified date, the creditor could take possession of their
land without having to go to court. With another year of bad
rainfall, Lek's parents could not repay the borrowed money in time,
and they lost their only possession and their means of livelihood
to their creditor in Chiengmai in 1976. We were told by the
village headman that this kind of story happened to several other
farmers in his village during that period.

After they lost their land, Lek's family lived in abject
poverty. The only consolation was that they still had a nice
house to live in. The family of seven gathered forest products
to live on, and in addition the parents worked as wage labourers
on their neighbours' farm for 20-25 baht a day during the harvest
season. But work was seasonal and they could not earn sufficient
to feed their family. In 1979 several villagers found that there
was a spare tract of land which was a part of the reserved forests
10 kms away. Lek's parents followed the examples of others, and
went to farm the land from scratch. They had to clear the land,
which was overgrown with trees. They burned the wood and made
it into charcoal. They sold some of this and brought some home
for use. The eldest daughter, Lek, was drafted in to help
clearing up the land, while the remainder of the family stayed
at home. With only three family workers they could clear only
one acre of land, and eventually this yielded them enough rice
for their subsistence. The family now had a regular source of
rice, but they had no other means to earn much cash. They could
not afford to send their children to school beyond the compulsory
elementary education which was provided for by the State. The
youngest two children did not even go to school. The parents
were too busy and too occupied with earning their livelihood to
spend any time on their children. They themselves did not have
much of an education.

Lek did not like working on the land at all. All her life she had known only poverty and hardship. She had seen some of the girls in the villages nearby who had gone to Chiengmai and Bangkok and had come back in their modern clothes looking very pretty and cheerful. She would like to go away and earn more cash to buy some of these nice clothes and have more money to buy food. In early 1980, an agent who had heard about Lek's poverty and the family's plight came to see her parents and offered a loan of money if they would agree to send Lek to work in Cholburi. This was a guarantee that the agent could always come back to recoup the girl if she ran away before she had worked long enough to pay off the debt. Lek went to work in a whore-house in Cholburi. She said she worked in a similar place to the one she was working in in Bangkok, but she went home because the business was not doing well and the owner closed the place down. We were told by her neighbours that her parents had notified the village headman that their daughter had been abducted by a man from another village and they wanted their daughter back. The deputy village headman then went to talk to the accused man. Apparently Lek was still only 16 and she was not supposed to be working in a bar, nightclub or joint. The agent then went and brought Lek back to the village. But Lek only stayed a day and went off to Bangkok straight away. Apparently this time the father went with her to see her workplace. He wanted to make sure that his daughter was in a good place. In fact, he wanted to know the location so that he could come to ask for more money - which he did two weeks after he had seen her off. Lek's story was confusing, and we could not get anything from her as she would say whatever the agent and her employers had instructed her to say. For instance, she said she was 18 while in fact she was only 16. When asked if her parents had signed a promissory note she said no. We found out from the deputy village headman who lived almost next door to her that her parents had signed a promissory note. Perhaps she did not lie in this case, perhaps she did not really know. But she certainly lied about her age.

I tried to find more details about the girl and the deal the agent had made with the family by talking to the village headman and his deputy, and by talking to the receptionist in the massage parlour in which she worked in Bangkok. From these interviews I gathered enough information from which to construct Lek's story

as follows.   When Lek was approached by the agent, the agent
offered to pay her parents 1,500 baht and asked the parents to
sign a promissory note to that effect.   But initially, the agent
only paid the parents a portion of 1,500 baht.   Lek was not
pretty and he was not assured of the income she would bring.
In addition, the family seemed rather hard up and would be prepared
to take whatever the agent said.   After a few months had passed,
the parents wanted the other half of the money.   The agent did
not want to pay, so the parents went to report to the village headman that their daughter had been abducted.   The deputy village
headman went to see the agent and asked him to bring the girl
back or else he would bring the police.   The agent then brought
Lek back to the village.   This time another deal was made.   The
agent would pay the rest of the money but Lek had to go to Bangkok
to work as she had not really worked off the debt.   Obviously
the agent had made another deal with the massage parlour in
Bangkok for a larger sum of money and saw this as a chance to
make more cash for himself.   The father insisted that he would
go to Bangkok too to make sure that their daughter was in a good
place.   He was paid the other half of the loan and returned home.
But he had to come back for another advance of 1,500 baht within
two weeks because his wife had fallen ill.   So the father was
after all quite a willing partner in this whole game and he only
reported to the village headman because he felt that he was cheated
by the agent.   He was probably right.   Had he not threatened
the agent with the force of law, the agent would not have paid him
the rest of the loan.   Lek's story is not uncommon.   The receptionist in Lek's massage parlour told me that more than half of
the girls who worked there (total of about 30) were "bonded girls"
in the same way that Lek was.   The amount the agent paid the
parents differed slightly, depending on the physical look and the
age of the girl.   He cited one case of a girl of 12 who came
because the parents sold her for 500 baht.   She was too young
to work, and was employed as an errand girl until she was old
enough.   The wife of the tailor who owned a shop opposite this
massage parlour said that she had several times seen girls from
the parlour with a bundle of clothes under their arms and tears
in their eyes.   Apparently an agent could get pretty rough on
the girls when they refused to work.   The receptionist said
that they were not really beaten up, but they would not be allowed
to go out of the building.

Had Lek had alternative employment in her village, her
parents might not have encouraged her to have such a fate.   It
could also be argued that had Lek's parents had access to good
credit or had the Government provided a better irrigation scheme
for the farmers, the family would not have to live in abject
poverty and drive their daughter to prostitution.

Suay and Taeng
(from Baan Son Ton Mue, Amphoe
Phang, Chiengmai Province, North)

Family profile:

Members of family	Age	Education	Occupation	Present place of work or residence
Father	44	P.4	Farmer	Chiengmai
Mother	40	P.4	Farmer	Chiengmai
Children:				
1. Daughter	20	P.4	Coffee-shop girl	Bangkok
2. Daughter	17	P.4	Help in the family	Chiengmai
3. Daughter	15	P.4	Help in the family	Chiengmai
4. Son	14	P.4	Help with family farm	Chiengmai

We knew a little about Suay and Taeng from the village headman before we went to interview their parents.   We asked the
village headman if he could show us some of the families whose
daughters have just returned from Bangkok after having worked as
masseuses.   The headman was very embarrassed but was willing to
co-operate.   He told us that Suay and Taeng went to Bangkok a
month ago with their eldest sister.   But three weeks after their
departure Taeng returned on her own.   Apparently she jumped over
the fence of her residence in Bangkok to come back home.   The
parents got alarmed about Suay and reported to the police that
their other daughter had been abducted to Bangkok.   The police

brought her back.   Somehow the parents dropped the charge and
things went on as usual.   To any other villagers, who did not
know the truth, Suay and Taeng came back from their holiday in
Bangkok so soon because they were sick.   They would go again as
soon as they were well.

Suay and Taeng and her family's stories were typical of a
farming family working on marginal land with traditional methods
of cultivation and with very small amounts of investment, so much
so that they could not earn enough income to maintain the family
subsistence and other cash needs.   They were forced to make use of
their children.   The children themselves would like to improve
themselves and to contribute to the family income.   But they
could not do that within the context of the village environment in
which they were born.   There was no alternative employment in
the village other than working as seasonal wage labourers in the
field and scraping about in the woods for forest products.   There
was not enough work as field labour to accommodate all the unemployed
and underemployed, and if no migrants had left, the glut in the
local labour market would have driven the wages down even further.
Gathering forest products would have been a possibility 20 years
before when the woods were still plentiful.   But with rapid
depletion of the forests in more recent years, villagers in remote
areas have quickly lost this important means of livelihood.   They
could not have moved out to earn a good salary in the city because
they did not have much education.   With four years of elementary
education, they could only read and write.   But Suay and Taeng
had one important asset.   They have beautiful skin and are very
pretty.   Thus an obvious occupation for them was something to do
with their beauty.

Suay and Taeng's parents came from poor landless families.
They used to live in a little thatched hut which was built on the
land of a distant relative.   When Suay was 12, her eldest sister
who was then 15 went to Bangkok with her aunt to work as a housemaid.   We learned from the conversation with the village headman
and from the father that Suay's eldest sister was in fact working
as a call girl in Bangkok.   She was in the international network,
as she went to spend a week or two with foreign customers sometimes.
The pictures of this sister and foreign men in tourist spots in
Hong Kong were shown to us during the course of our visit.   The
father also said proudly that his eldest sister in Bangkok usually

sent him 10,000 baht or so every three or four months. When the eldest daughter first went to Bangkok, she sent the family some money to build a new house. This was in 1976, and the house cost only 7,750 baht. It was not a large house but was much better than the old thatched hut that the family used to live in. The family living conditions improved greatly since the eldest daughter went to Bangkok. She later sent some money for father to buy a pair of bullocks (cost about 10,000 baht), to buy two acres of rice land, and to build a well for drinking water. This happened in the course of five years during the working life of the eldest daughter.

With two bullocks and two acres of land, the father could then till the soil for family subsistence. But the land must have been very bad soil indeed for he only earned something like 2,000 baht from it per year. This was hardly sufficient for a family of five. In addition, the father rented his bullocks out and worked in the neighbours' fields. This earned him another 1,300 baht per year. The family's monthly earnings, including rice for subsistence, was 275 baht, or 55 baht per person per month. This was far below the poverty line of 150 baht per person per month as defined by the World Bank for rural Thailand.

When Suay's eldest sister came to visit last summer she persuaded her parents to let her take the two teenage sisters to Bangkok with her. It was difficult to find out if there was any exchange of money on the occasion. Indeed we were not able to get the truth out of the girls or the parents. But from talking to the village headman and the parents we could piece the story together. What seems to have happened was that Suay's eldest sister had acted as an agent to bring the two virgin sisters to Bangkok in return for a rather large sum of money. But the sisters did not like it and one of them was courageous enough to jump over the fence and run away from the parlour. We had a chance to meet one of the girls, Suay. The other, Taeng, walked away quickly as soon as she saw us approaching her house. She probably thought we were the Bangkok agents coming back to look for her. The father received us well and asked the other daughter, Suay, to receive us as well. Suay was suspicious but consented. She did not utter a word during our visit. She looked very miserable and confused.

We learned a few things from our conversation with the father.
He told us that many girls from his village went South. His
daughter first went as a housemaid but now she worked in a
restaurant. She also travelled abroad. He said that girls who
went South were better off when they returned. They were also
prettier than those who remained behind. He thought it was a
good thing for the girls. Would he allow the other two daughters
to go South? Yes. One had the impression that the two younger
daughters would probably be persuaded to go to Bangkok eventually.
The elder sister would probably come to entice them again. We
felt that Taeng might get away as she seemed to have a mind of her
own and was quite courageous. Suay was much more submissive
and was the most likely victim.

Taeng and Suay's family is an example of a farming household
which did not improve its productive capacity even with a large
sum of remittances from the first daughter. The parents tried
to increase their standard of living further by pushing other
daughters out to prostitute themselves to bring in more money.

Ploy
(from Dok Kam Tai, Chiengmai, North)

The young district postal clerk at Dok Kam Tai took us to
see Ploy, the village pride. Four years before, when they were 13,
Ploy and her twin sister had been crowned the village beauty
queens at the annual summer fair. It was hardly a surprising
choice. Ploy was strikingly pretty, with a lovely complexion
and an attractive personality. The family also had two other
daughters - one younger and one older than the twins - and one
son. The eldest daughter and the son had had only four years
of elementary education while Ploy and the other sisters had
seven. The family had only about four acres of poor land and
used to live in a small hut. They found it difficult to bring
up so many children and to sustain their education. Their only
success was that all the daughters were decidedly beautiful.

At about the time of the twins' success in the beauty
contest, the elder sister went off to work in Bangkok as a call
girl. She soon got on the international network and went off
to service clients in Singapore and Hong Kong, besides the usual
business in Bangkok. The family produced photographs of her posh

Bangkok residence complete with its marble floors and swimming pool, as well as snaps of her travels abroad. In the compound of the family home she had built a lovely teak house at a cost of about 50,000 baht.

A year or two later there was a family crisis. The brother, Noi, and another cousin had got involved in the drug traffic, and were discovered by the police. In the shoot-out which followed, the cousin was killed and Noi was arrested. A large sum of money was needed to get Noi out on bail, and an even larger sum was required to ensure the right result at the subsequent trial. The money was raised by selling Ploy's sister to a Bangkok agent. The sum was reputedly ฿100,000, but this may well have been inflated. The usual sum for an ordinary girl with no special beauty was about ฿1,500, and a better-looking girl could command ฿5,000 or even ฿10,000 if she was a virgin. The highest sum we met with elsewhere was ฿50,000. It was possible that the sum paid for Ploy's sister was inflated either by family boasting or by local rumour.

Ploy's sister had subsequently built another house in the compound and would probably use it when she retired from her Bangkok work. A third house had been built and would probably be sold as a CKD wooden house in the future.

Ploy, meanwhile, was holding out against any pressure to go to Bangkok. She was determined not to go South and had been strengthened in her resolve by her twin sister, who had advised her not to go. As long as there were two other daughters contributing to the family purse then she had a good chance to escape. At the time of our visit she was learning sewing at the district occupational training centre.

The fate of Ploy's younger sister was less certain. She was equally pretty, though as yet not so well developed, and had stopped her schooling at the seventh grade. She already had ambitions to go to Bangkok and stay with her sisters. At the time of the visit she was 15.

Mai
(from San Pa Daeng, Amphoe
Vieng Pa Pao, North)

When we met Mai in her village she was 23 years old.   She
came from a landless family of two children.   Her parents used
to work as wage labourers in the neighbours' fields and live in
a little thatched hut built on the land of a distant relative.
They now live in a handsome, two-storey wooden house, which was
built by Mai at a cost of ฿40,000.   This amount she earned from
working for about three years as a call girl and later as a
masseuse in Bangkok.   When we met her she had been home for
three to four months, was rather unwell, and was trying to fit
back into the life of the village.   It was difficult to be sure
about Mai's true story because the story itself was clearly
complicated, and because Mai was obviously still involved in the
trade.   The outlines, however, are clear and they suggest a pattern which we could recognise in parts of the stories of other
girls.

When Mai was 17 she was sent to work as a housemaid in
Bangkok.   Many other girls went from the same village at around
this time because of the drought.   She was paid 105 baht a month
plus food, and this was hardly anything.   After two months she
was persuaded by an aunt who was already established in Bangkok
to abandon the housemaid job and start work as a call girl at her
"hotel".   Her aunt arranged the first customer and shared with
her the considerable proceeds.   She carried on in the trade for
about two years and earned enough to start building her parents
the new house.   But then her aunt's "hotel" had to be sold to
pay off a debt contracted by the aunt's gambler husband.   Mai
and the aunt both returned to the village.

The family was hit hard by the sudden loss of a steady source
of income.   Meanwhile, Mai was approached by a divorced man of
40 who wanted to marry someone who would help look after his
children and his farm.   Mai thought this was a good chance to
re-establish herself in the village and settle down.   However,
she only agreed to the match on the condition that the man would
promise to finish Mai's parents' new house.   He agreed, they
were married, and both Mai and her brother went to live on the
husband's farm.   But things did not turn out too well.   Mai and
her brother had to work very hard on the farm, but they never

received much money to spend and could see no progress on the
parents' house.   The husband appeared to have merely made an
advantageous contract to get two cheap labourers.   Mai became
pregnant, but also increasingly dissatisfied.   Yet if she was
to leave the husband, she would again need a means of livelihood.
At just the appropriate moment, she received a visit from the aunt.
By this time the aunt was working as cashier in a massage parlour
in Bangkok, and her visit was hardly casual.   Rather she was
talent-spotting.   The aunt suggested that she could return to
a much more glamorous life if she got rid of the child, left her
husband and went to Bangkok.   Even though she was already four
months pregnant, Mai managed to abort the child on her own by
squeezing it out.   It was painful but successful.   Her aunt
gave her an advance of 5,000 baht and went back to Bangkok.
Mai spent some weeks recuperating from the abortion and then
packed her bags and went to Bangkok.

The aunt's parlour turned out to be the same low-grade
whore-house in Suriwong where Lek worked.   It was hardly glamorous.
Mai was already sick from the after-effects of the self-administered
abortion, and the atmosphere of the new place of work hardly
matched up to the posher surroundings of her previous time in
Bangkok.   Moreover, she was now a "bonded girl" and thus could
not earn very much.   She was attractive and that pushed up her
earning power slightly, but the return per customer was still
only 15 baht.   Even that income was not assured.   According to
her, the owner of the house was a gambler and he never paid out
the full wage to which Mai was entitled.   Mai claimed that in
some months she earned 4,500 baht (this would mean an average of
ten customers a day and may be unlikely) but could receive as
little as 20.   Anyway, she was certainly working hard enough to
prejudice her already precarious state of health, and after
eight months had passed she became so unwell that she decided
to return home.   She must have earned reasonably well since she
had enough money to complete her parents' house.

The after-effects of the abortion were compounded by the
symptoms of VD, and Mai was in a pretty sorry state.   But she
at least had enough wit left to learn from her experiences and
to be instructed by the model of her aunt.   The economics of the
trade clearly favoured the agents, parlour-owners and other
intermediaries rather than the girls themselves.   Mai was now

clearly starting out on a new career as an agent.   Thus Mai was
a naive and rather confused village girl who wanted to help her
parents but who had little education or opportunity, other than
that presented by her aunt.   She became the victim of her own
vulnerability, and was setting out now to victimise those more
vulnerable than herself.

ж ж ж ж

    The main sources of migrant girls are the two poorest regions
of the country, the North and the North-east.   Within those
regions, the main catchment areas are some of the poorer villages.
Whether because of natural disadvantages, or because of the
in itably uneven quality, the economy of these villages is
especially precarious.   A sustained period of drought, the accumulated strain of advancing population pressure, the invasion of
outside interests with exploitative aims, can easily drive many
of the villagers across the margin of survival.

    Within these villages, many of the girls come from the more
vulnerable families.   Their backgrounds include landless migrants
like Taew's Laotian father, families whose ancestral land has
been decimated by subdivision, large families whose meagre assets
cannot support all the progeny, and small farmers or labourers who
are simply ill-equipped to cope with the shifting patterns of
economic fortune.

    Within these families, the women are not simply dependants.
They consider themselves as earning members of the household and
are considered likewise by the others.   It is not some sort of
helpless dependent status which ends them up in the business of
selling their bodies.   Rather it is the responsibilities which
they themselves feel.   The first charge on the money which they
earn is the remittance to their parents.

    The family also often operates as the agency for recruitment.
In many cases (not only those mentioned here), an aunt, sister or
cousin appears as the figure who inducts the girl into the business.
Other villagers, especially in the North, have a resigned attitude
to the business of "going South".   They recognise the economic
logic of the trade, and while the well-off and some of the
officials are ready to make moral judgements, the ordinary
villagers take a much more indulgent attitude.

The remittances have had a substantial effect on the outlook
of the villages.   Dok Kam Tai, for instance, now looks like a
prosperous place, for it is full of fine old houses and fine new
houses interspersed.   The impression of locally generated prosperity, however, is immediately punctured when one examines the
state of local agricultural production.   The vast change in
appearance often tends to obscure a more basic stagnation.   Much
of the remittance money has been devoted to improving the comforts
of the parental generation and to some extent of the generation
which follows.   Most of it has gone into building fine houses,
into sinking wells for providing drinking water, and for supple-
menting the day-to-day income for ordinary living expenses.
The postmaster in Dok Kam Tai noted that the remittances swell
in the months of March to June and November to January.   These
are the months of greatest activity in the agricultural calendar,
and the girls increase their remittances to cover the costs of
the wage labour which must be hired to sustain agricultural
operations.   Many of the families have had to replace their
daughters' labour with hired help, and the daughters are aware
of this substitution.   If they have not made enough savings to
send home for these seasonal needs, they may well turn up in
person to do the necessary tasks.   The migration is thus an
adjunct of the family's (and thus of the village's) agrarian
economy.   Little of the remittance, meanwhile, seems to have
gone into the expansion of productive assets.   Some of the
families have managed to buy a little land or acquire new bullocks,
but the over-all impression is that such expenditures are not
extensive.   The villages show little sign of attempts to use the
accumulated capital to import new technologies or productive
processes.   Most of the remittance is used to supplement the
meagre resources available for providing basic comforts like
housing, water and food.

This, of course, is not to be begrudged.   But since the
remittance is being used largely as current income rather than
as capital investment, the families and villages are not developing
any capacity to replace this source of earning.   This can easily
be seen on the small scale in the way that certain families have
acquired a vested interest in sending their daughters to the
South in series.   The traditional family system, in which the
youngest daughter would be expected to help the parents in their

old age, and in which daughters brought working men into the
family by marriage, predisposes parents to look at least as
happily on the birth of a daughter as a son.   But this sentiment
has certainly been strengthened.   Daughters now earn money
directly, and ease the problems of trying to squeeze an agricultural income out of an unresponsive soil.   It would be nice to
have sons, say the villagers, but daughters seem to be more
productive.

The growing dependence of certain families on this trade
has encouraged the growth of a breed of agents, talent scouts and
middle-men.   Parents can, in effect, mortgage their daughters,
and there are brokers who are ready at hand to carry out this
service.   Each of the villages which has a reasonable flow of
girls to the South has a number of agents.   Some of these are
girls who have themselves been through the mill, but others are
just men with a sharp eye for business.   The post offices
regularly send out messages such as "three bundles of goods
awaiting delivery on receipt of ฿10,000 each".   At the other
end the trade is clearly equally institutionalised.   Many of the
postal orders coming into Dok Kam Tai and destined for several
different families, originated from common names which probably
indicated agents at the Bangkok end who may have been forwarding
money which the girls had earned but perhaps never handled
themselves.

CONCLUSION

From one point of view, there is nothing very special about
the migration of the girls from Dok Kam Tai and elsewhere. Girls
from poor backgrounds are simply entering the oldest profession in
the world. But such a view misses all the important nuances of the
Thai case. To begin with, it obscures the fact that the girls are
not escaping from the ties of the family and low horizons of village
society. Rather, they are going out to support the family, and
perhaps also to improve their own position within the society of the
locality. They enter into this particular trade in response to the
obligations which they feel they owe to their family as part of a
customary role as earning members of the society. They may be
exploited by agents or damaged by ill health, but the fact that they
suffer in the same way as ladies of the night of the usual sort
should not lead to a conclusion that there is nothing specific and
unusual about the Thai girls.

Since the 1950s Thailand has opted for a particular strategy of
economic growth.[40] It has rejected the idea of using tight economic
planning, extensive controls, and all the usual paraphernalia of
"import substitution industrialisation" to build up a manufacturing
sector. Rather, it has kept the channels of international trade
as open as possible, and counted on private enterprise to achieve
economic growth by pursuing the comparative advantages which Thailand
enjoys. The country was set on this course as a result of a settle-
ment of internal and international politics in the 1950s. It should
be thought, however, that the pursuit of this strategy meant that the
society and economy would somehow be left to develop in a "natural"
way, without the kind of dedicated tampering which goes with rigorous
planning. The logic of Thailand's chosen path of development did
in fact demand that the economy be structured in a particular way.
First, as in most development strategies, the capital for urban
investment would have to be generated from agriculture. Aid and
foreign investment might provide a means to take out a mortgage on
the future, but the ultimate source of urban capital would be the
surplus skimmed off the primary sector. Second, the machinery used
for accumulating the surplus would be the international trading
economy. Thailand would turn the primary surplus into usable
assets by selling it on the international market. Third, the
resulting assets would have to be channelled into urban growth by
creating a series of appropriate incentives. In brief, this meant

ensuring high returns to urban investments, and providing a range
of "salary goods" (largely consumer imports).

Such a strategy involved some obvious techniques such as
minimising the restrictions on international trade and providing
packages of incentives to attract foreign and local investors to
sink money in urban enterprises.   It also demanded that the
Government ensure that the country maintain and strengthen the
"comparative advantages" which she enjoyed in the international
market.   In other words, the surplus goods which Thailand hoped to
sell to realise investible resources would have to be kept cheap
enough to be competitive.   To some extent this could be achieved
by investment in the local infrastructure (principally communications)
which transferred the primary surplus from the point of production
to the channels of international trade, from the farm to the port.
But beyond that, it also meant keeping the original prices of
tradeable primary products very low.

The Thai Government thus not only devoted a lot of aid funds
into developing communications and other parts of the country's
infrastructure, but also tried to keep primary prices down.   This
was not done to a great extent by obvious strong-arm methods, such
as price controls.   Mostly, it involved policies designed not to
channel too much social investment into the countryside, not doing
anything which would raise the expectations or the bargaining power
of the farmers, not allowing the rural interests to develop any real
political torque.[41]

In the 1970s the policy was extended slightly.   The reasons
for change were, firstly, that the country was running out of opportunities to augment the primary surplus by such methods without some
severe and possibly disruptive structural change in the primary
sector and, secondly, the terms of trade for Thailand's primary
sector were in decline.   Thus, another area of "comparative
advantage" was developed - that is cheap labour which could be made
available to local and international capital to produce manufactured
goods for sale in the world market.   In many ways this new direction
was an extension of the earlier policy rather than a fundamental
change.   The depressed rural sector provided a ready supply of
recruits into this labour force, and also harboured the "reserve army"
which kept down the price of labour, while the supply of cheap food
helped to minimise the cost of the "wage goods" demanded by this
labour force.   Thus, in the 1970s, the array of investment

incentives were embellished to encourage entrepreneurs to produce
specifically for export. Moreover, the qualities of Thai labour
were widely advertised:

> While the minimum daily rate in Bangkok is proposed to be
> 54 baht (US$2.70), it will be only 47 baht (US$2.35) in the
> Central and Southern regions and a mere 44 baht (US$2.20) in
> the North and North-east ... Thai workers have been found
> by many companies to be willing, dextrous, remarkably quick
> learners and conscientious, dependable workers ... Another
> point about Thai labour is that it is not militant. There
> have been many strikes, of course, but in general most dis-
> putes are settled amicably and indeed, this year, some of the
> country's labour leaders have said publicly that they will
> accept whatever wage increases the Government deems suitable.
> The reason for this stand is that labour leaders understand
> the present situation in the country and have decided that
> unity is more important than large wage increases.[42]

This strategy of development, pursued now for over quarter of
a century, has had important consequences for the evolution of Thai
society. First, it has established Bangkok as a rapidly growing
primate city dominated by an urban middle class which monopolises
wealth and political influence. Second, it has condemned the
countryside to a course of expansion without change. Better
communications and marketing systems conveyed the pressure of world
demand into the countryside and induced a massive expansion of
primary production. But this was achieved without substantial
technological change or extensive social engineering. Basically,
more and more farmers were doing more and more of the same thing.
The rewards increased, but in per capita terms the increase was
small and out of all proportion to the importance of the primary
surplus in the over-all strategy of economic growth. Moreover,
expansion was unevenly distributed. In part, the unevenness was
geographic.

In the Central Plain, where there was a reasonable network of
communications and marketing established in the colonial period,
and in those parts of the other regions which had good access to the
new markets and roads, the benefits flowed most easily. It was a
different matter in a village at the end of a long dirt road, or
on the other side of a craggy hill. In part, the unevenness was
social. Expansion benefited those who already had a good grasp
over productive assets (particularly land). Meanwhile, for those
who did not have the social and geographic advantages, the process
of expansion merely squeezed them closer and closer towards the
margin. One element of this process is nicely summed up in the

statistics on forests which serve as the last resort of the poor.
Between 1947 and 1977, the area under forests diminished from
90m acres to 42m acres.[43]   Much of that which was left was on the
slopes of distant hills.   The margin was rapidly being erased.

But the chief effect of the development strategy was not simply
that it swelled the city or that it constrained the countryside
within a pattern of growth with stagnation.   Rather, it was the
combination of these two.   The gap in incomes and opportunities
between city and country gaped enormously wide.   This provided the
setting for the migration.   On the one hand, the urban earner could
buy the services of a girl at a price which was relatively cheap
within his personal budget.   The Thai customers of the massage
parlours extend through a wide range of social classes and income
levels.   At the bottom end of the market, at 15 baht per trick,
they include labourers and taxi drivers.   On the other hand, for
the girls from a poor rural background the migration gave them an
earning power which was simply astounding relative to normal rural
budgets.   A couple of years of work would enable the family to build
a house of a size and quality which few people in the countryside
could hope to achieve on the earnings of a lifetime.

A similar economic rationale extended to the international
arena.   When Thailand began to place more emphasis on the export of
goods and services produced by cheap urban labour, there was one
sector in which the largely unskilled labour force already enjoyed
a distinct "comparative advantage" without the need for any further
investment incentives.   The marketing of this particular sector
more or less looked after itself.   The "comparative advantage"
stemmed in part from the availability of girls, and that depended on
the recent history of the development of the trade.   But it also
stemmed from the favourable price.   The agencies which marketed
sex tourism stressed not only that the bar of the Grace Hotel was
full of girls, but also that they would cost so little.   The
weakening of the Thai relative to some foreign currencies in the
late 1960s and early 1970s also reduced the real price the tourist
had to pay for the special services.

It is within an economic system structured in this particular
way that the actions of the migrant girls must be understood.   They
were not fleeing from a family background or rural society which
oppressed women in conventional ways.   Rather, they were engaging
in an entrepreneurial move designed to sustain the family units of

a rural economy which was coming under increasing pressure.   They
did so because their accustomed position in that rural society
allocated them a considerable responsibility for earning income to
sustain the family.   The returns available in this particular
business, rather than in any other business accessible to an
unskilled and uneducated person, had a powerful effect on their
choices.   Our survey clearly showed that the girls felt they were
making a perfectly rational decision within the context of their
particular social and economic structure, and they could not escape
from it.

The migration is thus an intrinsic part of Thailand's economic
orientation.   Thailand's strategy depends internationally on
accepting a dependent and vulnerable role in the world economy, and
depends internally on keeping the primary sector in a dependent and
tractable state.   A business which sets girls out of the poorer
parts of the countryside and sells their services to the urban
earner and to the foreign visitor is merely the mirror image of this
hierarchy of dependence.

There are, of course, many other poor countries in a similarly
dependent state, pursuing comparable strategies of development and
exhibiting an equally wide gap between urban and rural incomes.
Few of them, however, have developed a "trade" which comes close to
rivalling that of Thailand.   Yet it is no good seeking an explanation for this in any eternal characteristics of Thai culture.
There is nothing especially "loose" about Thailand's rural women.
Indeed, there are signs that rules about courtship and marriage were
strict and understood, and that the kind of extra-curricular activity
which must be common to virtually every rustic community in the world
was conducted with a discretion and decorum that demonstrated an
above average sensitivity about the maintenance of standards of
public conduct.

The trade has been successfully oriented to an urban and international market and embedded deeply into the structure of the Thai
economy.   It provided a means of survival for poor rural families,
and it helped earn the foreign exchange to cover import costs.   The
North-eastern girls gradually began to lose the prominent position
in the trade as Northern girls were prettier and clearly more in
demand in Bangkok.   Whatever the reason, it appears that the
migration from the North-east may be static or in decline, and that
the villagers of the North-east are already beginning to rebuild

their aversion to such a business.   For the North, however, the business is still on the increase.   Whatever the geographical origin of the girls, there is no sign that the migration is going to tail away.   The infrastructure created by the Viet Nam War has been firmly established within the over-all strategy of economic development.   Young girls are one of the rural resources to be exploited for the sake of the balance of payments and urban growth.   Sexual tourism is one of the services available through the open door of the open economy.

The fact that the massage business has become an integral part of the Thai economy (were it to be drastically reduced, there would be unemployment and balance of payments difficulties) undermines any realistic possibility of short-term cures.   Thailand already has a number of organisations dedicated to refurbishing the moral character of the massage girls, and also a number of more sensible institutions which try to help them out of trouble.   But no amount of agitation is likely to change things while the cost incentives remain the same, and the opportunities for alternative employment are so limited.   There are signs that individual girls use their earnings to help their sisters and their daughters to escape the trade.   Some girls devote their earnings to providing education for their sisters and daughters, and to setting up small businesses. But if some families can use the massage earnings to clamber up one of the ladders of escape, there are other families which will slide down the snake of misfortune.   Besides, the evidence from places in the North suggests that families and villages are accumulating a vested interest in the business.   Sister follows sister.   Neighbour follows neighbour.   The only real solution is a long-term one, and it lies in a massive change in the distribution of income between city and country, and in a fundamental shift in Thailand's orientation to the international economy.

ACKNOWLEDGEMENTS AND NOTES

Acknowledgements

Abha Sirivongs Na Ayuthaya, who was going to be my collaborator, was unfortunately unable to take part because of other commitments, but made many useful suggestions. Among my colleagues at the Faculty of Economics at Chulalongkorn University, Thiranart Karnjanaaksorn, accompanied me on the upcountry trips, Supachai Manaspaibool and Prescha Piamphongsant helped with the questionnaires, and several others assisted with the interviews in the parlours in Bangkok. Dr. Thepanom Muangman allowed me to see the results of his study, Charuk Suwanpanich of the NESDB provided upcountry maps, Astri Suhrke helped with the pre-test of the upcountry survey, Suzy Greuter shared with me her first-hand experience of massage and her second-hand knowledge of the international network, and Jacques Amyot, Nisa Xuto and Kraisak Choonhavan provided me with useful information. A number of helpful officials smoothed the path of the upcountry survey, especially Dusit Patamanant of Phang, without whose help it would not have been possible to reach some of the remote areas. Christopher Baker assisted in editing, and Supaporn Thonggitviroj did the typing. I am grateful to all of these people for their considerable help, but most of all, I am indebted to the girls and the families who were the victims covered in this survey.

Notes

N.B.:   1 baht = US 5 cents (approx.)
The units of rural administration in Thailand are as follows: baan (hamlet); tambon (village); amphoe (district); and jangwat (province).

[1] J.F. Embree: "Thailand - a loosely structured system", in American Anthropologist, Vol. 52 (1950). See also L. Sharp: Siamese rice village: a preliminary study of Bangchan 1948-49 (Cornell Research Centre, Thai Niyom Building, Samyod, Bangkok, 1953) (later published as Bangchan: Social history of a rural community in Thailand, Ithaca, NY, Cornell University Press, 1978); H.K. Kaufman: Bangkhuad: a community study in Thailand (Locust Valley, New York, J.J. Augustin for the Association of Asian Studies, 1960); J. de Young: Village life in modern Thailand (Berkeley and Los Angeles, University of California Press, 1955).

[2] S.H. Potter: Family in a Northern Thai village (Berkeley and Los Angeles, University of California Press, 1977), p. 20. See also J.M. Potter: Thai peasant social structure (Chicago, University of Chicago Press, 1976).

[3] A. Turton: "Matrilineal descent groups and spirit cults of the Thai-Yuan in northern Thailand", in Journal of the Siam Society, Vol. 60 (1972); S.J. Tambiah: Buddhism and spirit cults in Northeast Thailand (Cambridge, Cambridge University Press, 1970).

[4] S.J. Tambiah: World conqueror and world renouncer (Cambridge, Cambridge University Press, 1976).

[5] Chit Pumisak: Chomna Sakdina Thai (The true face of the Thai aristocracy) (Chomrom Nang-sue Sangtawan, Bangkok, 1974).

[6] G.W. Skinner: Chinese society in Thailand: an analytical history (Ithaca, NY, Cornell University Press, 1957); R.J. Coughlin: Double identity: the Chinese in modern Thailand (Hong Kong, Hong Kong University Press, 1960); F.L.K. Hsu: Under the ancestors' shadow: Chinese culture and personality (New York, Columbia University Press, 1948).

[7] Thamrongsak Ayuwatana: Rachasakul Chakri Wong (Members of the Chakri Dynasty), Part I (Bhanakij Trading, Bangkok, 1972).

[8] Thak Chaloemtiarana: Thailand: the politics of despotic paternalism (Bangkok, 1980), pp. 338-339.

[9] Wolfgang Wehner: "American involvement in Thailand", in Journal of Contemporary Asia, 1973, pp. 292-305.

[10] Bangkok Bank: Monthly Review XIV, 10 (1973), p. 666.

[11] Tourist Authority of Thailand.

[12] "Sex tourism to Thailand", in ISIS International Bulletin, 13 (1980); and Maria Mies: "Prostitution tourism in South-east Asia", Berlin, Free University of Berlin, Mar. 1978 (unpublished paper).

[13] Calculated from figures in Bank of Thailand: Statistical Bulletin, Dec. 1979, Table III.2.

[14] Week (Bangkok), 23 June 1980, p. 12.

[15] See, for example, Suporn Koetsawang in "Abortion on the upsurge", in Bangkok Post (Bangkok), 11 Aug. 1980.

[16] Ministry of Health, Department of VD Control, 1979.

[17] Thepanom Muangman et al.: "Report of a study on education, attitude and work of 1,000 massage girls in Bangkok with special reference to family planning, pregnancy, abortion, venereal disease and drug addiction", (unpublished paper in Thai, Bangkok, 1980).

[18] "From northern girls to Bangkok prostitutes", presented at the Conference for Cultural Unity of the Four Regions, Thammasat University, 25-27 Jan. 1980.

[19] Thepanom, op. cit. It may be interesting to note, by way of comparison on income levels, a university lecturer (government employee) with Ph.D. publications and several years of teaching experience receives a salary of just over 4,000 baht a month.

[20] Interviews with textile workers, Bangkok. At present some companies put the retirement age for women at 40.

[21] Thepanom, op. cit.

[22] Interviews conducted in May-June 1980.

[23] Thai Rath (Bangkok), 20 June 1980, p. 5.

[24] "What do we know about land problems?", in Varasarn Setakit lae Sangkom (Economic and Social Journal), published by the National Economic and Social Development Board, (Bangkok, Jan.-Feb. 1980), p. 9.

[25] By 1969, six military airports were built in Thailand by the United States Government, four of which are located in the Northeast region.

[26] See footnote 24.

[27] J.M. Potter: Thai peasant social structure, op. cit., p. 56.

[28] ibid., pp. 78-79.

[29] Abha Sirivongs Na Ayuthaya et al.: Village Chiengmai (Bangkok, Chulalongkorn University Social Research Institute, 1979).

[30] Oey Astra Meesook: Income, consumption and poverty in Thailand, 1962/63 to 1975/76, World Bank Staff Paper No. 364, November 1979, p. 62.

[31] ibid., pp. 52-54.

[32] Thailand, National Statistical Office: 1970 population and housing census, subject report no. 2: migration (Bangkok, 1978), p. 9.

[33] ibid., pp. 23-24.

[34] ฿200 round trip.

[35] Oey Astra Meesook, op. cit., Chapter 4.

[36] Report on the socio-economic conditions of Amphur Dok Kam Tai, Chiengmai Province, Research and Evaluation Division, Community Development Department, Ministry of Interior, Bangkok, 1973.

[37] 1.6 acres would provide the family with rice alone, but would not yield any surplus to sell or barter against other foodstuffs and other products.

[38] Abha Sirivongs Na Ayuthaya et al., op. cit.

[39] For want of a better word, I have used this term - a coffee-shop girl - rather than prostitute in order to distinguish this kind of relatively free-lance and independent job from the pimp-dominated situation of prostitution in Europe and elsewhere.

[40] See Pasuk Phongpaichit: "The open economy and its friends: the development of Thailand", in Pacific Affairs (Fall, 1980).

[41] See Pasuk Phongpaichit: Economic and social transformation of Thailand, 1957-76 (Bangkok, Chulalongkorn University Social Research Institute, 1980).

[42] Bangkok Post, Supplement, 4 Aug. 1980 (Bangkok): "The labour situation", p. 21.

[43] "What do we know about land problems", op. cit., p. 15.

Women, Work and Development
(ISSN 0253-2042) – Some earlier titles in the series

Unpaid work in the household: A review of economic evaluation methods,
by Luisella Goldschmidt-Clermont   WWD 1
This monograph examines the various economic approaches used to evaluate unpaid work in the household. It analyses the strengths and weaknesses of each method, particularly in relation to social values and labour market conditions. The monograph provides a useful starting-point in a field deserving further investigation.
ISBN 92-2-103085-7   17.50 Sw. frs.

State policies and the position of women workers in the People's Democratic Republic of Yemen, 1967-77, by Maxine Molyneux   WWD 3
This monograph, which is the first survey of women in Democratic Yemen, analyses the main changes that have occurred in the position of women as a result of state policies and economic development, and discusses the measures implemented by the State as regards women's legal status, their political involvement, their education and their employment.
ISBN 92-2-103144-6   17.50 Sw. frs.

Women in Andean agriculture: Peasant production and rural wage employment in Colombia and Peru, by Carmen Diana Deere and Magdalena León de Leal WWD 4
According to the prevailing interpretation of census data, the Andean region of South America has a male farming system. This monograph challenges that interpretation by showing that rural women participate actively in agriculture, both within peasant units of production and in the rural labour force. Census data suggest that the participation of rural women in agriculture has decreased in recent decades; but the findings of this monograph imply that it may in fact be increasing.   ISBN 92-2-103106-3   20 Sw. frs.

Women workers in the Sri Lanka plantation sector:
An historical and contemporary analysis, by Rachel Kurian   WWD 5
Plantation labour systems display certain similarities across regions, cultures and crops, and they have some common historical roots. Commonly, too, the position of women workers in agriculture in many countries is unfavourable. In this monograph the author, on the basis of her field research, traces the particular evolution of the plantation system in Sri Lanka and portrays the nature and conditions of work by women on tea, rubber and coconut plantations. Suggestions are made for improvement. ISBN 92-2-102992-1   20 Sw. frs.

Fertility, female employment and policy measures in Hungary,
by Barnabás Barta, András Klinger, Károly Miltényi and György Vukovich   WWD 6
Has women's employment in fact been an important factor affecting fertility? Are there other factors and policies contributing to lower fertility? These and other questions are examined in this detailed study of Hungary, which not only gives demographic and employment data for the Hungarian population as a whole but also provides interesting information on KAP (Knowledge, Attitude and Practice of Family Planning) surveys, panel surveys of marriage cohorts, and time budget studies.   ISBN 92-2-103624-3   15 Sw. frs.

Craftswomen in Kerdassa, Egypt: Household p   ction and reproduction,
by Patricia D. Lynch with Hoda Fahmy   WWD 7
This monograph describes the contributions of   in an Egyptian community to subsistence activities and handicrafts production   e changes in labour processes which increasingly push women into less rewardi   f work. It discusses the ways in which women's work is related to child-bearing ar   ...ng and the significance of children's work for increased productivity.   ISBN 92-2-103625-1   15 Sw. frs.

Fisherwomen on the Kerala coast: Demographic and socio-economic impact of a fisheries development project, by Leela Gulati   WWD 8
Some 30 years ago, fishing and fish preservation activities in three villages in Kerala (India) were mechanised. Except where women benefited directly from social infrastructure facilities built into the project, they were left out of the project design. This monograph shows how these changes affected the lives of women from fishing households, both economically and demographically.   ISBN 92-2-103626-X   20 Sw. frs.